AN INTRODUCTION TO

Embroidery

ANNA GRIFFITHS

AN INTRODUCTION TO
Embroidery

ANNA GRIFFITHS

Grange
BOOKS

To all my keen embroidery friends
who helped me on this project

A QUINTET BOOK

Published by Grange Books
An Imprint of Grange Books plc
The Grange
Grange Yard
London SE1 3AG

This edition published 1995

ISBN 1-85627-861-1

This book was designed and produced by
Quintet Publishing Limited
6 Blundell Street
London N7 9BH

Creative Director: Peter Bridgewater
Art Director: Ian Hunt
Designer: James Lawrence
Project Editor: Caroline Beattie
Editor: Anne Wilkinson
Photographer: Andrew Sydenham

Typeset in Great Britain by
Central Southern Typesetters, Eastbourne
Manufactured in China by
Regent Publishing Services Limited
Printed in Singapore by
Star Standard Industries (Pte) Ltd

11–15 Marion Appleton. **18, 19** designed and worked by Pauline Brown. **20** designed and worked by Anna Griffiths. **25** Audrey Francini (photo Martin Gostelow). **26** The Helen L Allen Collection. **27** Episcopal Museum, Bayeux (photo Giraudon). **28–31** designed by Anna Griffiths, worked by Pat Round. **32** Muriel Best. **33** worked by Frances Duncan. **34** lent by Stephen Molnar. **35** Vicky Lugg (left), Muriel Best (right). **36–7** designed by Anna Griffiths, worked by Wendy Walker. **38–41** designed and worked by Anna Griffiths. **43–4** designed by Anna Griffiths, worked by Wendy Walker. **52** designed by Thea Gouvernour for Michael Whittacker Fabrics (David Hyde Photography). **53** designed and worked by Anna Griffiths. **54–5** designed and worked by Frances Duncan. **56–7** designed and worked by Lucy Griffiths. **58–9** designed and worked by Wendy Walker. **61** (top) Stitch Sampler: Pat Round; (bottom) Horse: designed and worked by Anna Griffiths. **62–63** designed and worked by Caroline Beattie. **64** Lesley Woodward (left). **65** interpreted and worked by Wendy Walker. **68** designed and worked by Anna Griffiths. **70** designed and worked by Pauline Brown. **71** Textile Conservation Centre, Hampton Court Palace. **75** Jean Moncrieff. **77** designed and worked by Caroline Beattie. **78–9** designed by Anna Griffiths, worked by Betty Fanning. **80–1** needlecase designed and worked by Anna Griffiths; cushion front designed and worked by Louise Beattie. **82–5** Shelley Faye Lazar. **86** designed and worked by Caroline Beattie. **87** Jane Waldman. **88–91** designed by Anna Griffiths, worked by Erika Brisland. **92–3** grey needle case designed and worked by Brenda Scholes; part-worked sample by Wendy Walker.

Contents

Introduction

Hand embroidery is a satisfying occupation that millions of women (and some men) enjoy, but starting off can be daunting if you have never approached it before. This book gives you a selection of basic stitches to practise, examples showing how the stitches can be used and projects to do in each area in the hope that you will go on to create your own individual work. But first, let us look at the history of embroidery.

The desire to ornament and embellish fabric surfaces seems to have been with us a very long time. According to legend, when Menelaus took Helen home from Troy after the Trojan wars, they stopped in Egypt where the rulers presented Helen with an embroidery basket as a token of their esteem, proof that embroidery was a serious activity even then. Traditionally, women have always been associated with embroidery. Matilda, the wife of William the Conqueror, is reputed to have worked the Bayeux Tapestry in the 11th Century; Mary Queen of Scots in captivity embroidered exquisite pieces and Marie Antoinette in France made lace from the threads she pulled from sacking in her cell while in prison. These women, and many millions more, have experienced the tremendous pleasure, satisfaction and even comfort that embellishing fabric with stitches can give.

Embroidery has to be done with a needle. According to the Roman historian Pliny the Elder in the first century the Phrygians were the first people to use a needle to embroider. Early needles were made from bones, quills or bronze. Steel needles were in use by the 16th Century, introduced by traders from China.

The purpose of embroidery in the past falls into many different categories:

Religious embroidery– The Bible makes numerous references to decorated materials in gold and silver on priestly

White Linen Sampler
Below *This 'sampler' was probably the work of a professional itinerant needlewoman and embroiderer to show her skills to potential employers. Even moderate sized houses employed a woman for a certain amount of time each year to do mending of household linens, embroidery and some less important dressmaking. The sample is of very fine linen and shows tucks, gathers, shadow appliqué and embroidery, a gusset, bound button and buttonhole, different types of seams and hems, frills, needle and made lace insertion, darning, eyelets, drawn thread work and needle edgings.*

Danish Cross Stitch
Right *This fine example of counted cross stitch comes from Denmark and was probably worked to commemorate the wedding of the girl, Karen Andersen.*

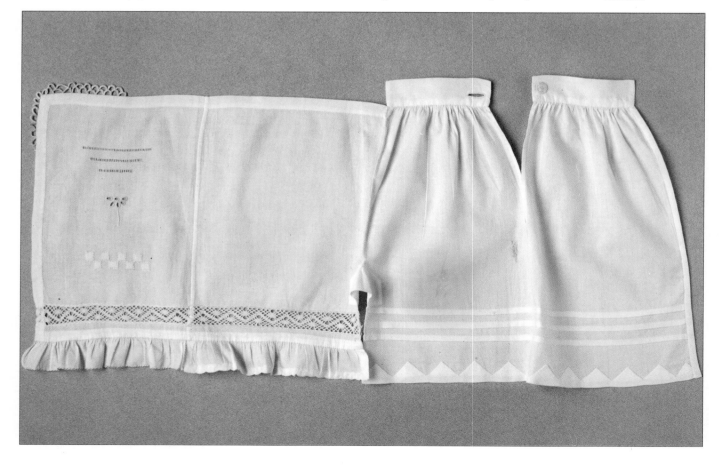

robes, tabernacle veils and clothing. In Europe, it was patronised by the churches, with many of the patterns and techniques dispersed by returning crusaders and warriors. Religious themes were combined with flowers, fruit, birds and animals for use by the church and in heraldry. This declined after the 14th century and the Black Death, although Henry VIII made an extravagant prestigious spectacle with his army in 1520 at the 'Field of the Cloth of Gold'. The heraldic garments worn over armour and the trappings for the horses made such an impact that it is recorded to this day by reference to the splendid gold embroidery.

To denote rank and power – By using extravagant embroidery on clothing with precious metals and jewels. It reached its peak in Europe in the 16th and 17th centuries.

To record events – As in the Bayeux Tapestry, showing the life of King Harold and the conquest of England by the Normans. It is comparable to a graphic account in a present day newspaper. In the 17th century it became customary for young girls to work samplers or 'examplars', which usually give the name and age of the person who worked it as well as the date it was worked. Samplers were supposed to be pieces of work to practise different stitches, but they often included a scriptural text to improve the young girl's mind. Samplers were also worked by adult women, especially if they were hoping to be taken on by a large household as the seamstress/embroiderer. They needed to show all their different sewing skills as well as embroidery stitches.

For functional and practical use – To strengthen fabrics used on furniture and for decorating and adding weight to wall-hangings and curtains, which helped to keep some heat in the cold stone-walled mansions. This was particularly strong during the Reformation in Europe, when embroidery moved from the ecclesiastical domain into general use. Great householders always had a professional embroiderer in their retinue of servants.

In recent history, embroidery has had a sporadic journey – enthusiasm for domestic needlework increased under Queen Anne (1702–1714), but then waned until 'Berlin Work' appeared around the 1800s and became very popular. This system gave us our first 'kit'! Mr. Philipson of Berlin had the idea of copying 'Old Masters' on graph paper. He allocated one stitch to each square and indicated the colour to be used on woven canvas, often using bright colours produced by new chemical dyes.

Along with this revival was an ongoing enthusiasm for 'fancy art needlework' or embroidery done with threads on china ribbon (silk ribbon ⅛ in/3 mm wide) depicting fish-scales, feathers, beads and silk gauze etc.

In the late 1890s the Arts and Crafts Movement brought in traditional and modern designs worked in wool, silk, linen or velvet. Design was influenced by William Morris and Lewis T. Day, often based on Elizabethan and Jacobean designs, using soft, natural colours based on vegetable dyes.

In the 1920s stitches were re-discovered for their own sake. Slowly, into the 1960s, they gained importance, challenging the printed and woven fabrics that were mass-produced. Here in the late 1900s, with a shrinking world, we are fortunate to have at our disposal a wealth of fabrics, threads and information from every continent, to give us the greatest choice ever. All we need to add is our own enthusiasm and willingness to learn from the past and we can discover and form the future.

BASIC EQUIPMENT

You need very little in the way of equipment to start embroidery; as you go further into it you will add to the range of threads and fabrics when you take on new projects. To start with you just need:–

a selection of needles, a pair of fine-pointed embroidery scissors, fabrics, such as medium-weight calico or cotton, and threads like stranded cotton or pearl cotton. With these items you can practise the stitches before you start on a project.

Threading the needle – A needle-threader is useful for fine needles. Pass the wire loop through the eye of the needle, place the thread through the loop and then draw the loop back through the needle, pulling the thread with it. Alternatively, use the loop method illustrated.

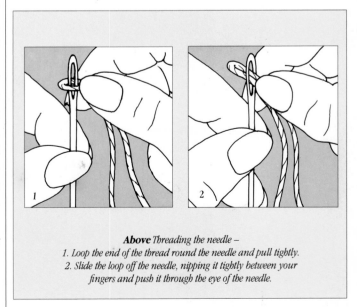

Above *Threading the needle –*
1. Loop the end of the thread round the needle and pull tightly.
2. Slide the loop off the needle, nipping it tightly between your fingers and push it through the eye of the needle.

Right *Nineteenth century Indian embroidery, worked in chain stitch in cotton on a wool ground.*

Starting and finishing the thread – When you start stitching, do not use a knot as this may show through the finished piece or make a bump on the right side, especially if the work is to be framed or will be seen both sides, as in our towel project. Anchor the thread by making one or two tiny back stitches in a space that will be covered as the stitching progresses. Alternatively, leave a tail of 2 in (5 cm) of thread which can be darned in later. If you are continuing to work an area which is partly stitched, anchor a new thread by sliding the needle under the wrong side of a group of stitches, securing about 1 in (2.5 cm) of the thread underneath them. To finish a thread, slide the needle in the same way under a group of stitches and cut off the loose end of thread.

Each area in this book will give you specific advice and suggestions for fabrics, needles and threads to use. However, you may like to know more about the types of needles and threads that are available to embroiderers.

Needles – Needles for hand embroidery are of three types: crewel, chenille and tapestry. They have longer eyes than do needles used for plain sewing, to make threading a thick thread easier. All needles are numerically graded from fine to coarse, the higher numbers being the finer needles. Exact choice of needle is largely a matter of personal preference, but the eye of the needle should accommodate the thread easily and should be the right size to draw the thread through the fabric or canvas without pulling it out of shape. You will soon discover by 'feel' which size and type of needle suits the work you are doing.

Crewel needles – sizes 1 to 10 – are sharp, medium-length needles with a large eye and are used for fine and medium-weight embroidery on plain-weave fabrics.

Chenille needles – sizes 14 to 26 – are also pointed, but are longer, thicker and have larger eyes than crewel needles and are used with heavier threads and fabrics.

Tapestry needles – sizes 14 to 26 – are similar in size to chenille needles, but with a blunt end instead of a sharp point. They are used for canvaswork and embroidery on even-weave fabrics; the blunt end separates the threads of the fabric to pass through, whereas a sharp needle would split them.

Right *Detail from a Chinese coat, worked mainly in fine satin stitch, with stem stitch worked on top of the completed leaves for the veins and closely-packed French knots worked in the centre of the open flowers.*
The selection of colours used has been carefully thought out. The tips of rust on the flowers and leaves add a little excitement to an otherwise monochromatic scheme.

Above *A selection of materials and basic equipment needed to start embroidery. From the top: tapestry wool, stranded cotton, coton à broder, fine embroidery scissors, gold thread, a selection of needles, felt, canvas (double-thread and mono canvas, plastic canvas), Aida fabric, pearl cotton.*

Threads – Embroidery threads are made in a wide range of weights and colours. Some are twisted and must be used as one thread, while others are made up of several strands which can be separated and used singly, or put together in different weight or colour combinations. For cross stitch embroidery or plain or even-weave fabric, the following threads are suitable:

Stranded cotton – a loosely twisted, slightly shiny, six-strand thread which can be separated for fine work. A good all-purpose thread with an extensive colour range.

Pearl cotton – a twisted two-ply thread with a lustrous sheen, which cannot be divided. It comes in sizes 3, 5 and 8, 3 being the heaviest, and in a good range of colours.

Soft embroidery cotton – a tightly twisted 5-ply thread, fairly thick and with a matt finish. It is used as a single thread on heavier fabrics.

Coton à broder – a tightly twisted thread which is similar to pearl cotton, although softer, finer and with a less lustrous finish.

Stranded pure silk – a seven-stranded, shiny thread which can be divided. It comes in an extensive colour range including many brilliant shades not available in stranded cotton. It is also available as twisted thread, in a much narrower colour range. Pure silk is difficult to work with and must be dry-cleaned.

For canvaswork, wool yarns are usually preferred as they are most hard wearing, but often stranded cotton, silk or pearl cotton is introduced for highlights. For articles that do not require a hard-wearing finish, such as pictures, any of the previous threads can be used on their own. Crewel and Persian wools are suitable for even-weave fabrics, providing the fabric is loose enough to allow the thread to pass through easily, without shredding or fraying.

The wools most widely available are:

Crewel wool – a fine 2-ply wool for delicate canvaswork, available in a wide range of subtle colours. Two, three or four strands can be used together on coarse canvas.

Persian wool – a loosely-twisted three-strand wool which can be divided. Each strand is slightly thicker than crewel wool and the colours are brighter.

Tapestry wool – a tightly-twisted 4-ply wool used singly on coarse canvas.

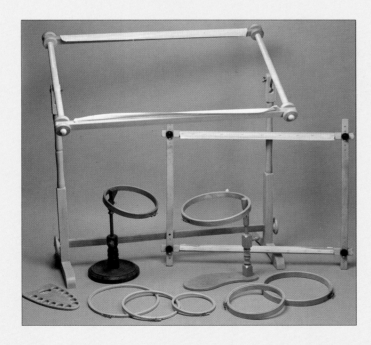

OTHER EQUIPMENT

Left *Frames are required for some kinds of work. The ones in the picture are used in different ways. The largest one (back) has the work laced on to canvas tapes; the other rectangular one can have its height adjusted and can be dismantled. The small dark wood frame can be stood on a table and is for finer work. The frame with the kidney-shaped foot is pushed underneath you as you sit, and your weight anchors it so that you have both hands free to work with. The hoops in the front are held in one hand and worked with the other and the wooden palette with holes is used to keep threads tidy.*

Apart from the basic items referred to already, there are a number of general sewing aids that would be useful – a pair of good dressmaking scissors, a thimble, a tape measure, ordinary sewing needles and thread for tacking and a box of good sharp pins.

Free Embroidery

This area embraces a wide range of stitches and type of work on virtually every kind of fabric. The one element common to them all is the lack of restriction in the way the stitches can move over the surface, unlike counted thread work.

Each special section will give advice on fabrics and threads, but in general, the important thing to remember is to match the weight of the thread and needle to the fabric. If they are too heavy, the weave is distorted and the thread pulls it out of shape. Firmly woven fabrics that allow the thread to pass easily in and out are the best choice.

Above *Long and short stitch is used to make the petals of the front pansy, and buttonhole stitch for the two in the middle. A sense of distance is achieved by using a single strand of cotton and spaced straight stitches for the flower and leaves at the back.*

Above *This small sample looks more complicated than it is, being
mainly buttonhole stitch in different weights of thread and in
varying directions and combinations.*

River at Giverny

Right *This is a free interpretation of the River Seine at Giverny, where the painter Monet lived for many years. The panel was inspired by a visit to his famous garden there and the many pictures he painted of that part of the river.*

The main areas were achieved by overlaying net and fine fabrics to make the different parts of the woods and river. These were then caught down with a few stitches, ready for the main embroidery. French knots and stem stitch in wool and cottons were used to suggest the trees overhanging the river, with arrow heads above them to add extra texture. The water and reflections are worked with straight stitches in various colours of cotton and wool.

FREE EMBROIDERY STITCHES

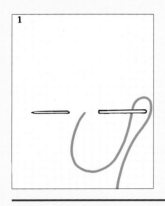

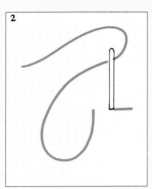

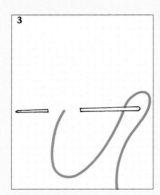

Back Stitch *is used extensively for outlining. Working from right to left, bring needle out on line, make a short straight stitch to right and bring needle out on line to left – the same distance from the starting point (1). Insert needle at starting point (2) and repeat along line, working with even stitches close together (3).*

Stem Stitch *is used mostly for lines and stems but it can also be worked in rows close together, as infilling. Bring needle out, make a short back stitch on line and bring out in middle with thread below needle point (1). Repeat along line, placing each stitch close together (2). For wide stem stitch insert needle at a slight angle, increasing angle for wider effect (3).*

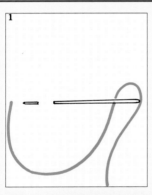

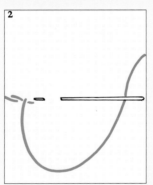

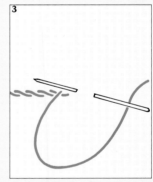

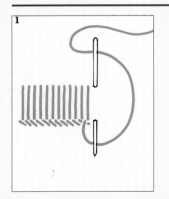

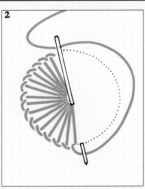

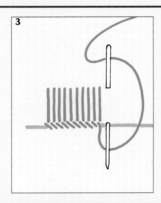

Buttonhole Stitch *is ordinarily used to give a firm edge to handmade button holes, but it is also used for cutwork and free-style motifs. It is worked with the stitches placed close together (1). For a buttonhole stitch wheel, take the needle through the same central hole, spacing the outer stitches evenly apart (2). For a firm edge, work over a row of split stitch (3).*

Double Running Stitch *is used mostly as an outline stitch in free-style embroidery. It is worked in two operations. Begin by working evenly spaced running stitches on the traced line. Then using the same coloured thread, working running stitches in the spaces left. Unlike back stitch, double running stitch is reversible.*

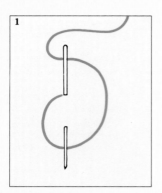
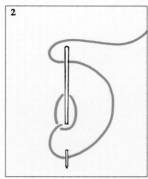
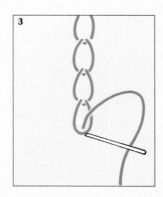

Chain Stitch *can be used to outline or fill areas. Bring needle out and make a straight stitch downwards inserting needle at starting point. Pull through with loop under needle point (1). Repeat, inserting needle where thread emerges (2). Finish row with a small stitch over last loop to secure (3).*
Detached Chain Stitch *is formed in exactly the same way but each loop is secured by a small stitch before the next loop is made.*

Cross Stitch *is best worked on evenweave fabric. Working from right to left, bring needle out on bottom line, take it to top left and bring out directly below on bottom line. Complete a row of diagonal stitches (1). Working from left to right, complete crosses by making diagonal stitches in the opposite direction (2). For a single cross, work from bottom right to top left, then from bottom left to top right (3).*

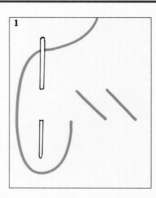
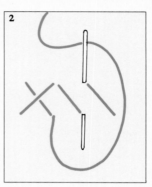
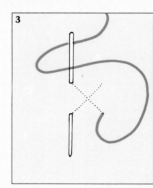

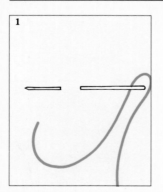
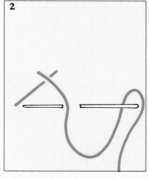
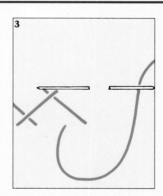

Herringbone Stitch *is used for lines and borders. Working from left to right, bring thread out, take it diagonally upwards and make a short back stitch on top line (1). Repeat, making a similar stitch on bottom line, bringing needle out directly under starting point of stitch above (2). Continue in this way along the row, working evenly spaced stitches (3).*

Satin Stitch (upright) *is used mostly as a line or border stitch. Begin on bottom line and make a short upright stitch (not longer than 3/4 in (2 cm). Bring needle out close to starting point (1). Make a second stitch close to the first (2). Complete the row, keeping an even tension (3).*

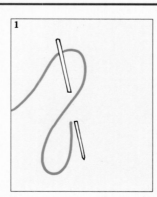
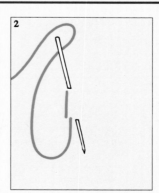
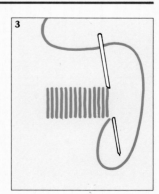

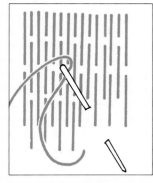

Long and Short Stitch *also known as plumage stitch and shading stitch. Long and short stitch is a variation of satin stitch that gives a gradually shaded effect. It is also used to fill an area which is too large or irregular to be covered neatly by satin stitch and can be worked on plain or even-weave fabrics and on canvas. The first row is made up of alternately long and short stitches which closely follow the outline of the shape to be filled. The subsequent rows are worked in satin stitches of equal length.*

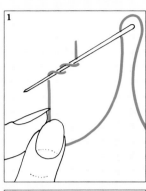

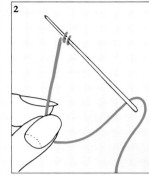

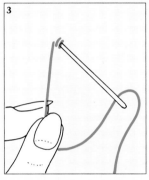

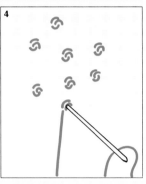

French Knots – *can be worked separately or close together. Bring needle out, and holding thread firmly with left hand, twist needle twice around thread (1). Tighten the twisted thread (2) and insert needle close to starting point (3). Pull needle through to back of fabric leaving a well-shaped knot on the surface. Repeat as needed (4).*

Bullion Knot – *can be used as a filling or line stitch. Bring needle out, insert it a short distance away (the length of the bullion knot), and pull through needle point only. Twist thread around point five or six times (1). Carefully pull needle through without disturbing the twists (2). Pull working thread and coils tight (3) and reinsert needle at same point to keep knot flat (4).*

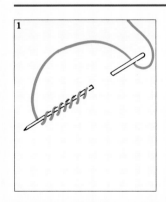

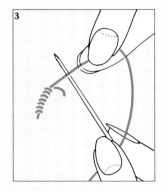

Blanket Stitch – *as its name implies, is used as an edging stitch, but it can also be used for borders and outlining in both free-style and counted-thread embroidery. Working from left to right, bring needle out on bottom line. Insert it on top line, to right, and bring out directly below with thread under needle (1). Repeat along row (2) and finish by inserting needle on bottom line (3).*

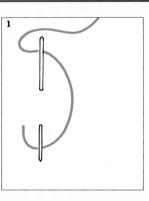

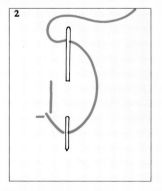

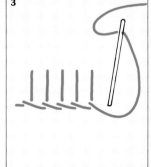

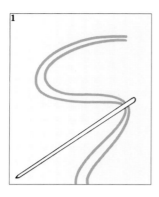

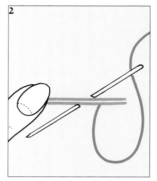

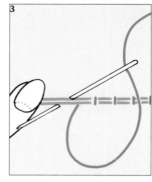

Couching – *use for outlining or infilling. Bring out thread to be couched at right (1). Hold down to left. Bring out couching thread below. Make small upright stitch over laid threads and bring needle out below, a little to left (2). Continue to work evenly spaced stitches (3). Turn threads at row end and couch with horizontal stitch (4). Turn work round. Place stitches between those of previous rows (5).*

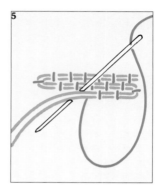

Jacobean Couching or Trellis
Lay evenly spaced threads (vertical and horizontal, or diagonal) across the design shape, and tie down all intersections with a different thread. The tiny tie or couching stitches can be slanting stitches or small crosses. Trellis work is a pretty filling for open leaf or flower shapes.

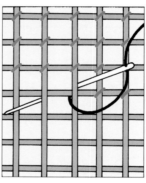

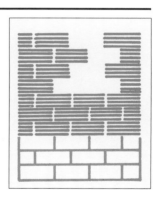

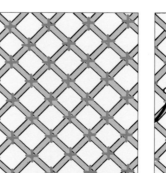

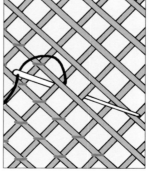

Brick Stitch
Arrange small, rectangular blocks of horizontal or vertical satin stitches in staggered columns, to give a brick wall effect. Useful for filling large areas.

CREWEL WORK

Crewel work is a form of ornamental needlework. 'Crewel' refers to the type of wool used, a special worsted yarn of two twisted strands. The characteristic soft colours were derived originally from home-made dyes. These shades can be found today, as well as stronger, brighter, modern colours.

Old specimens of crewel work were often inspired by nature, depicting flowers, fruit, insects, birds and animals. In the Stuart period in England, the famous East India Company brought shiploads of painted cottons into Europe from the Orient. The images inspired embroiderers, with the Tree of Life, the scroll, the wave and the hillock and fantasy trees and flowers, often highly stylised and far removed from nature, affecting the designs of the period. They became the handwriting that we associate with crewel work today.

Right This piece of American crewel embroidery by Audrey Francini shows a variety of different stitches which create eye-catching textures and unusual effects. The whole piece has a very lively feeling to it.

.... H i n t s & S u g g e s t i o n s ....

1 Any fabric that will not pucker may be used, but a neutral ground of unbleached linen or twill is traditional.

2 Buy a selection of crewel needles: a large one will be needed for double threads, a fine one for minute details. Thread the needle with the cut end of the wool from the skein, not too large, to avoid fraying and fluffing.

3 Crewel yarn should be used.

4 Try not to pull the stitches too tightly, as this will make the fabric pucker.

5 To put the design on the fabric, either draw free hand with an embroidery pencil, directly on to the fabric, or trace the design on to a piece of thin tracing or draughtsman's detail paper. Turn it over and, with an embroidery transfer pencil, go over the outline. Then place it on the fabric, with the original drawing upwards, and iron it, so that the dye is released. This is ideal if you want to repeat the design more than once.

Opposite page *This is a piece of nineteenth-century American crewel work, embroidered in 1851. The designs developed in the United States were often influenced by those prevalent in England, but were lighter, leading to a considerable amount of plain ground fabric. This was partly due to the fact that wool was not easy to obtain, so the preferred stitches were those which used as little as possible: laid work was popular. This beautiful, fresh floral design is executed in rich yet subtle colours.*

Left *A section of the eleventh-century Bayeux Tapestry, illustrating cavalry men going into battle at Hastings in 1066. It is mostly worked in wool couched on a linen ground.*

27

SMALL PANEL OF HORSES
IN CREWEL WORK

This crewel work panel was inspired by a print of a wall painting brought back from Sweden. During the 18th and 19th centuries travelling artists went from village to village offering their services. This could take the form of portrait painting for individuals wealthy and important enough to want it, or wall paintings that were worked as a frieze on one or more walls. The stylised drawings of the horses in the panel used here were typical of the naïve decorative approach of the work done during this period.

Materials needed:

A piece of fine wool challis finished size 14 in × 17 in (35 cm × 18 cm)

Crewel wool in six colours: deep burgundy red was used for the outline plus yellow ochre, mid-grey, light and dark orange, and white

Crewel needles

A frame to work on

Tracing paper and embroidery marking pencil or ordinary lead pencil

To begin the work:

Make a tracing of the design and place it underneath the wool challis fabric – you should be able to see it quite clearly. Draw carefully around the outlines with a lead pencil or an embroidery pencil. Attach the fabric to a frame by oversewing the top and bottom to the tapes. You will also need to lace the sides of the fabric to the side bars of the frame.

Swedish horses frieze
Right *The completed panel.*

Right *This is the beginning of the Swedish horses frieze. The design has been drawn on to the fabric and the outlines worked in burgundy crewel wool in stem stitch. The manes have been started using a combination of long and short stitch and satin stitch.*

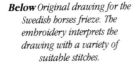

Below *Original drawing for the Swedish horses frieze. The embroidery interprets the drawing with a variety of suitable stitches.*

One strand of crewel wool is used throughout. Start by working the horse outlines in stem stitch. You can now decide whether you want to keep to the suggested stitches or put your own in. Here is the list of stitches used in the picture:

Horse outlines – all horizontal lines

Saddle outlines – stem stitch

Manes – long and short or satin stitch

Bridles – chain stitch

First saddle on the right – couched trellis

Second saddle – zig-zag edging with blocks of vertical stitches

Third saddle – cross stitches with an extra stitch across

Fourth saddle – rows of zig-zag edging with horizontal stitches

Tails – stem stitch worked closely together

Patterns on bodies of two horses – stem stitch

Flowers – blanket stitch and French knots

Eyes – two small black beads sewn on with black sewing cotton

The words and numbers were worked with one strand of embroidery cotton.

You can do more embroidery patterns on the bodies if you wish, perhaps equally spaced French knots or detached chain stitches. The horse would look equally effective worked much larger on heavier fabric, perhaps a slightly-textured linen. You must decide whether one strand of crewel wool is heavy enough for the outlines, and whether more solid filled-in patterns would be more suitable.

29

Right *The original sources of inspiration (from central Sweden) for the Swedish horses panel are shown with the embroidered interpretation. This picture shows how the wool ground has been sewn to the canvas tape on the embroidery frame. The fine wool that was used had to be kept very taught while being worked.*

CREATIVE FREE EMBROIDERY

Even with a limited stitch vocabulary you can create interesting effects: some wonderful work is traditionally done in India with just chain stitch, as illustrated in the introduction.

__Right__ Rows of running stitch using different thicknesses of twisted silk, in tones of one colour, are used to build up a design. The stitches range in size from very small ones, in fine thread, to larger ones, in thicker thread. In places the stitches are worked in close rows to give density and weight, in contrast with the more openly stitched areas.

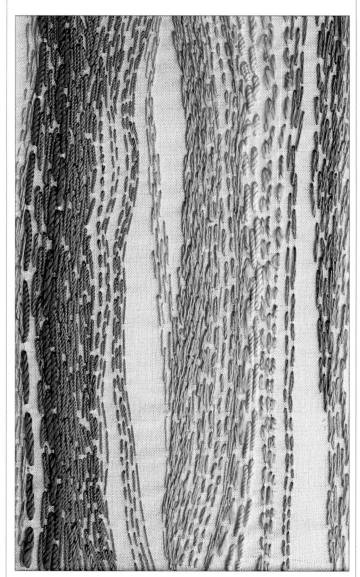

As an experiment in creative stitchery, find a photograph or magazine cutting and take a small section from it. Select one or two basic stitches and re-create on your fabric an impression of the image you have chosen. Try packing stitches together for dense areas and opening them out for lighter ones. Change the direction of the stitches for a change of angle. Experiment with different thicknesses of thread and colour, overlap them, add more on top in a different colour. You can soon see a textural pattern emerging.

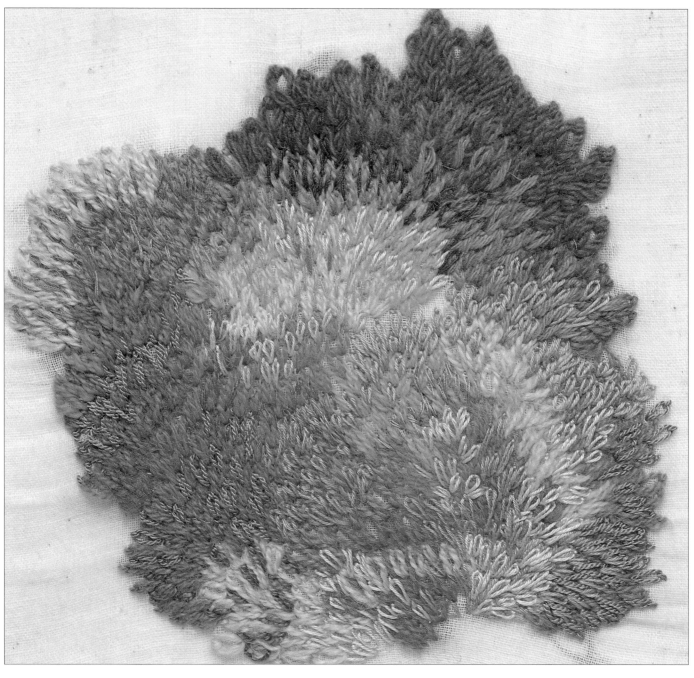

Above *Detached chain stitch has been worked in many different weights and types of thread, massed together in this sample. The effect is like an abundant herbaceous border.*

Almost anything goes in this area, both in fabrics to work on and threads. Furnishing fabric departments and stores often have remnants of interesting textured fabrics for sale. It is worth buying them for future use. Look for interesting threads – these might be knitting yarns, raffia, string, ribbons or leather thonging, as well as conventional embroidery threads.

When you are working on embroidery in this area, you are well advised to put the fabric on a frame or hoop, unless the fabric is very unstructured and would deteriorate by being stretched very tightly.

Above *This 80 year old cloth from Hungary is worked in satin stitch with small amounts of stem stitch. It looks, at first, a very regular, formal design, but it has been worked in a very free way and small differences of size and colour are not that important, for the whole thing looks well integrated. Variations of these images have been used in Hungarian embroidery for centuries.*

STITCHES FOR TEXTURE

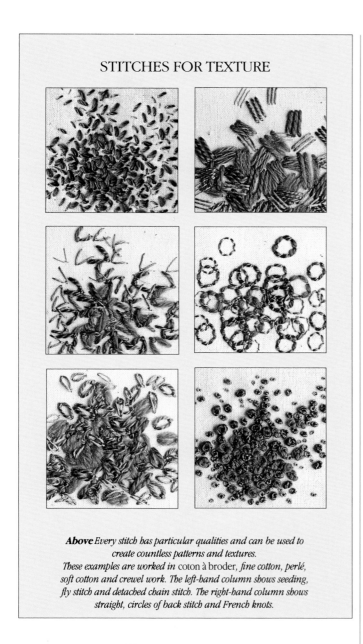

Above *Every stitch has particular qualities and can be used to create countless patterns and textures.*
These examples are worked in coton à broder, *fine cotton, perlé, soft cotton and crewel work. The left-hand column shows seeding, fly stitch and detached chain stitch. The right-hand column shows straight, circles of back stitch and French knots.*

CREATING TONES

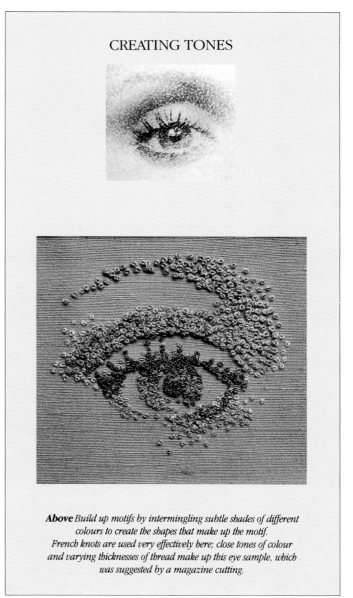

Above *Build up motifs by intermingling subtle shades of different colours to create the shapes that make up the motif.*
French knots are used very effectively here; close tones of colour and varying thicknesses of thread make up this eye sample, which was suggested by a magazine cutting.

SHADOW WORK

This is a delicate form of embroidery, oriental in origin, traditionally worked in white on white. It was often combined with surface stitchery and open work in the past, and sometimes with fabric shapes applied to the fabric to give a larger area of 'shadow'.

Herringbone or double back stitch is one of the stitches used. It is worked so that the crossed threads lie at the back of the work. These show through the semi-transparent fabric to form the shadow effect. Modern work often uses coloured threads which appear as pastel tints on the right side of the work. Shadow work is not really suitable for articles that are used regularly and therefore need laundering.

Suitable fabrics – Transparent and fine fabrics are essential, so lawn, organdie, chiffon, muslin and voile are best.
Threads – Stranded cottons, stranded pure silk.
Needles – Crewel, fine, small.

SHADOW WORK
EASTER CARD

Before attempting this delicate design, practise the stitch technique first. You only need three stitches for the design, the most important being herringbone stitch. Take a piece of transparent fabric, such as fine voile or sheer crystal organza, clamp it firmly in a small embroidery hoop; thread a fine pointed crewel needle with two strands of embroidery cotton in a medium tone, and work little blocks of herringbone on top. Turn it over to see whether the stitches are showing

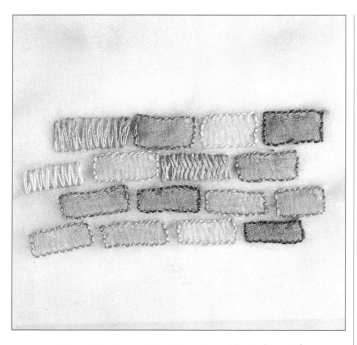

***Above** A practice sample experimenting with herringbone stitch worked on alternate sides to perfect the stitch.*

through on the other side neatly and evenly, and examine the effect of the shadow of the thread colour. Experiment with both pale and strong colours to see how they look. You can work the herringbone on the underside if you prefer, try alternating blocks on top and blocks underneath. When you have perfected this stitch, go on to the card project.

Materials needed:

A piece of sheer crystal organza – 8 in × 8 in (21 cm × 21 cm)

Stranded cotton in deep violet, mid-violet, sage green and yellow

An embroidery hoop

Fine crewel needles

A blank card with an oval or rectangle shape cut out (to mount the finished work – available from craft shops and department stores)

To begin the work:

Trace the pattern on to a piece of thin paper or greaseproof paper. Place the organza on top of the tracing and draw the outline on to the fabric with a pencil, making sure you do not distort the fabric.

Put the fabric into the embroidery hoop, ensuring it is really tightly fixed. Work each violet petal separately in herringbone stitch with two strands of cotton, finishing each one off on the back by passing the thread through a few stitches as neatly as possible before cutting it. Work the leaves in two halves, one half either side of the central vein. The stems are worked by making a row of evenly-spaced running stitches and returning back over the work to fill in the

spaces created (double running stitch). This way you will not get a shadow behind the stem, just a crisp single line. The centres of the violets can be made with either a single French knot or five small running stitches forming a circle.

Take the finished piece of work and cut it to fit the card size. Place it in the window of the card, checking to see that it does not hang over the edges. Spread the window surround on the back with a suitable glue, and position the embroidery in place. Make sure the image is central before pressing firmly down to fix.

Suggestions for other uses for the 'Violets' Shadow Work

1 Use the violets down the front of a chiffon or voile blouse or on a voile collar.
2 Reverse the shadow work colours by working light colours on a dark voile or organza evening stole or scarf.
3 Place the violets on the edge of a wedding veil, worked in white or cream with tiny seed pearls for the flower centres.
4 Make a sheer throwover tablecloth and embroider the violets in each corner, using it over a conventional cloth.

***Above** The pattern or the violets design can be traced over and used in any size.*

Above *Shadow work violets: the finished work mounted into a card.*

ADDRESS BOOK COVER

The design is loosely based on a band of decoration on an old vase and worked on felt, but you could use any closely woven fabric as long as you allow extra at the top and bottom for a turning to neaten the edges.

Approach this design with an open mind, choose the colours you like and work the stitches that you think are interesting. The design outline gives stitch suggestions, but you do not have to stick to them.

Materials needed:
Book to cover
Tracing paper
Felt or closely woven fabric
Dressmaker's carbon paper
Embroidery threads

To make the book cover:
Take the book you want to cover, place a piece of paper over the book, tucking it inside the back and front covers, allowing at least a third of the depth of each cover to go on the inside. Mark the top and bottom dimensions as well as the length. Straighten the paper out, then measure and draw the shape accurately, not forgetting to indicate where the spine of the book goes. Place this paper pattern on to your fabric and cut to size, marking the spine and the turnovers for the ends. Trace the design on to tracing paper or very thin paper. Place the fabric on a hard surface with a sheet of dressmaker's carbon paper on top; place the tracing on top of that; pin in place at the outer edges; draw round the outlines with a hard pencil – this will transfer the design through the carbon paper. Use blue or red carbon paper for light fabrics and yellow for dark ones.

Select the colours you want to use. Start the design by working the two vertical outside lines and the main curves in chain stitch. Now the rest is up to you – use whatever stitch you want, from the stitches already described, to fill in the rest. When it is finished, blanket stitch the turned back edges together and continue with blanket stitch right along to the other turn back. Continue this way until complete.

Suggestions for other uses for the design

Spectacle case cover or bookmark
Horizontally across a canvas or fabric bag

Right *Trace outline pattern for the address book cover.*

Opposite page *An embroidered book cover, based on a design from a pot. The pattern could be enlarged for bigger books.*

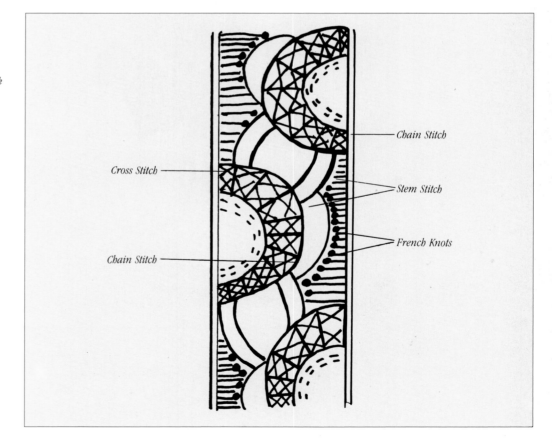

Chain Stitch

Cross Stitch

Stem Stitch

French Knots

Chain Stitch

EMBROIDERED
BERET AND GLOVES

Materials needed:
A felt beret and matching gloves
1 skein of coton à broder
A sharp pointed needle that will take the thread easily
2 pieces of tracing paper or tissue

To transfer the design, first trace the pattern outline on to the paper. Lay the beret on a hard surface, place the tracing on top in the position where you want the embroidery and pin the outer edges of the paper through on to the beret. With sewing thread in a contrasting colour, tack through the traced lines. When the design outline is completed, gently tear away the paper leaving the tacking. Using *coton à broder*, work the outline in chain stitch. Complete the flowers with two bullion knots for the centres, work the other dots with the same stitch.

The same method of transferring and working the design is used for the gloves, so make sure you do not tack through the whole glove. If the gloves are knitted, you will find that the design will not be reproduced so accurately and might be slightly different on each hand; which is only proof that they are hand embroidered!

.... *Other uses for this design* ....
1 Down the front edges of a knitted or fabric jacket, in a matching colour, or perhaps using a shiny or metallic thread for an interesting effect.
2 On the bottom of fine net curtains, using a matching coloured thread. They will appear as a more solid outline if you use a heavier thread than the fabric.
3 Use the flower motifs overlapping in two different colours on one corner of a plain wool scarf or shawl.
4 Round the bottom edges of a short evening jacket, replacing the centres with pearl or shiny metallic beads.

Although the design is very simple, you can use it in many different ways. You could change the scale, use different threads, overlap the shapes or separate the flowers and scatter them. Try working the flowers in other outline stitches instead of chain stitch.

Right A bought beret and gloves are given the personal touch with a small amount of easy embroidery.

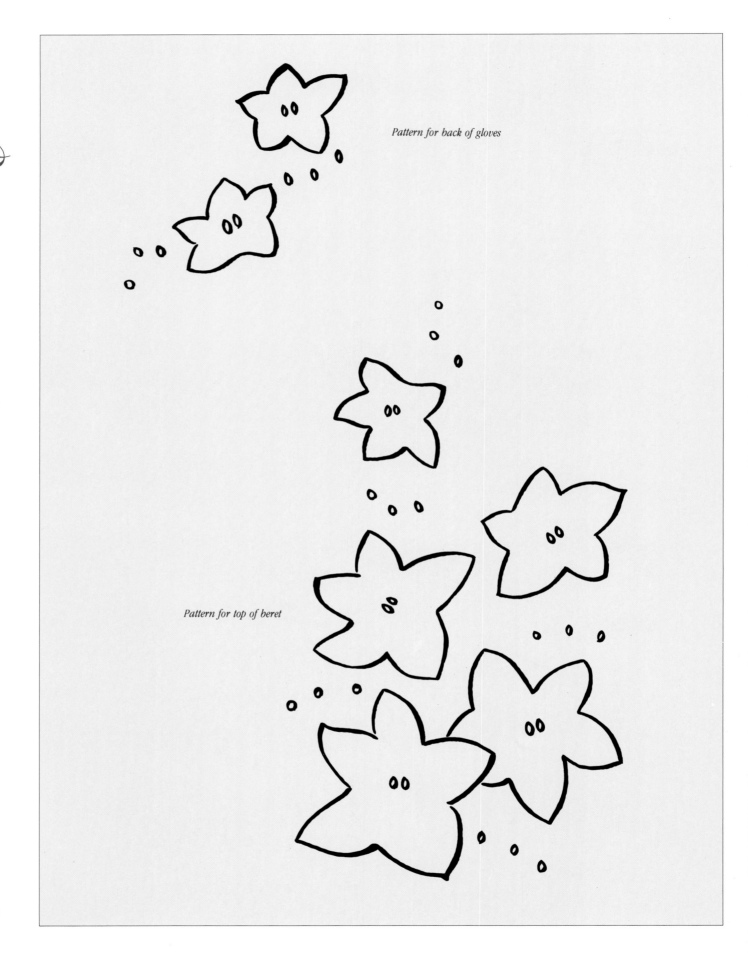

Pattern for back of gloves

Pattern for top of beret

PLACE MATS

Left *Trace outline drawing for the Beret and Gloves project.*

Only four stitches are used in this design for place mats – chain, buttonhole, stem and satin stitch. The design is best worked in an embroidery hoop. Whether you choose a hand held one or the 'sit-on' type, it should be bound round with cotton tape on the inner ring, fastening it tightly with masking tape or a few stitches. This prevents damage to the fabric and helps to keep it securely in place. Place the fabric over the inner ring with the design facing upwards, then place the outer ring over it and tighten the screw. Work round with your hands pulling the fabric tightly and evenly until it makes a slight drum sound when you tap it.

To make the place mats:

For each one you will need *a piece of fabric, medium-weight is best, about 14 in × 18 in (35 cm × 45 cm). (Finished size 12 in × 16 in (30 cm × 40 cm).)*

Four skeins of embroidery cotton (stranded or coton à broder) – one of each colour

A fine crewel needle that will take your chosen thread

Tracing paper and dressmaker's carbon paper

Below

Place mats can be made quite inexpensively to match your own colour scheme and they make unique presents. It is wise to keep the embroidery fairly flat, as too many large knots, for example, will make an uneven surface and the plates will rock.

43

To start the design, iron the fabric flat. Trace off the pattern on to the tracing paper – if you want it larger or smaller a local photo-copying service will do this for you, or use the squares to enlarge or reduce it yourself.

Place the fabric to be worked on a firm surface, place the carbon paper on top and the design tracing on top of that. Pin the layers together around the edges, with a tracing wheel or hard pencil go round each shape. This will transfer the image on to the fabric.

Put the fabric in the embroidery hoop and begin the stitching, following the guide to the stitch types. You may need to re-position the fabric in the hoop for the straight chain stitch lines. Lightly press the fabric on the wrong side after you have removed it from the hoop. Trim the excess fabric away from all sides, leaving 1½ in (4 cm) for the turnings.

Decide if you want to turn under the seam to the finished size and hand-stitch it on the back, or turn it to the front and stitch it down with a decorative stitch. Alternatively a straight machine-stitched line could be used.

This design could be scaled down and used on the corners of matching serviettes, or repeated in the original size on the four corners of a tablecloth.

Right *This is an exuberant example of free embroidery made up of satin, buttonhole and stem stitch in pearl cotton. The mat comes from Portugal where designs like this are on sale everywhere.*

Below
Trace outline for mats project.

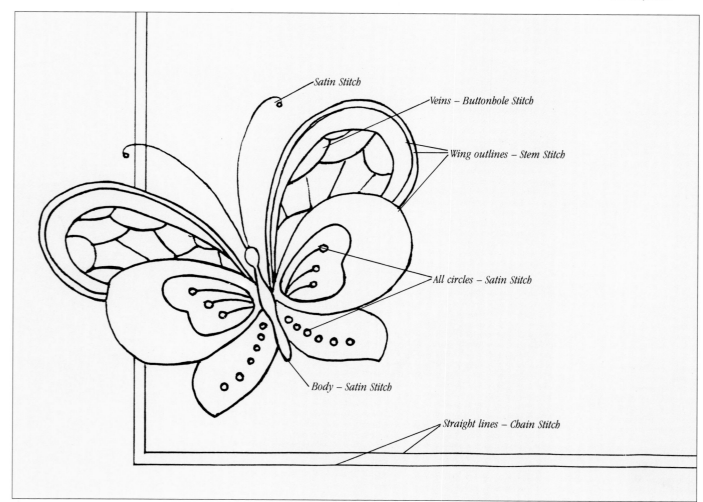

Satin Stitch

Veins – Buttonhole Stitch

Wing outlines – Stem Stitch

All circles – Satin Stitch

Body – Satin Stitch

Straight lines – Chain Stitch

Counted Thread Embroidery

As the name implies, counted thread work needs to be executed on an even-weave fabric with the same number of threads in the warp and the weft. The threads are counted as the number of stitches are worked. This may sound a bit daunting to a beginner, but once you practise for a time, you will see how the stitches become part of the fabric, as you are using the structure of the fabric to place the stitches. You can design simple patterns on squared paper, the squares representing the warp and weft threads of the fabric.

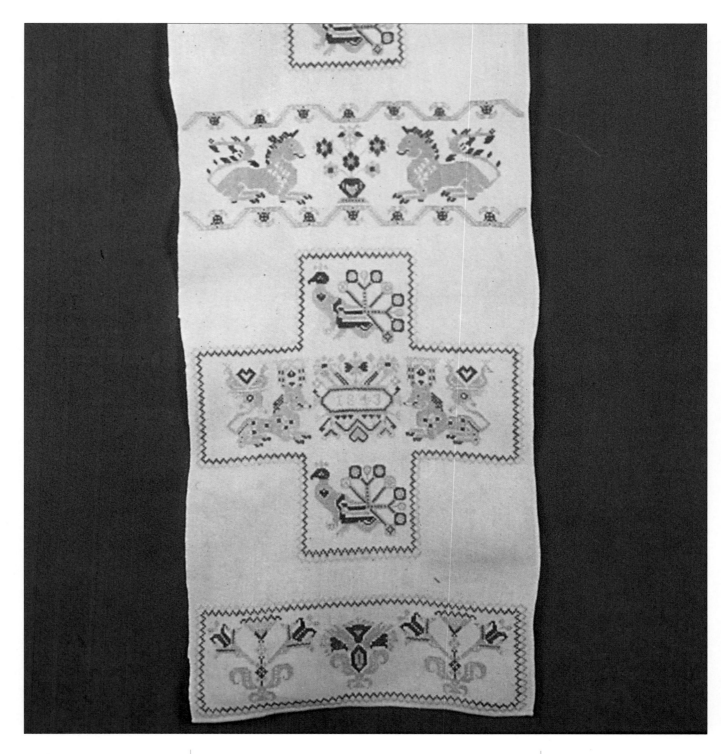

Above A Danish counted cross stitch table runner worked on linen, featuring stylized birds and animals.

As the name implies, counted thread work needs to be executed on an even-weave fabric with the same number of threads in the warp and the weft. The threads are counted as the number of stitches are worked. This may sound a bit daunting to a beginner, but once you practise for a time, you will see how the stitches become part of the fabric, as you are using the structure of the fabric to place the stitches. You can design simple patterns on squared paper, the squares representing the warp and weft threads of the fabrics.

COUNTED
THREAD STITCHES

 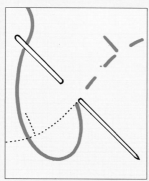 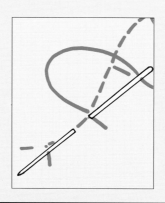

Holbein Stitch *is a variation of a double running stitch.*
Begin as for double running stitch, making a series of short even stitches on a traced line. Turn work round and work running stitches in the spaces. To work offshoot stitches, bring the needle out on line, make a short right angle stitch, bringing the needle out at starting point ready to continue stitching (2). Complete the row, turn work and fill the spaces as before (3).

Fly Stitch *is a looped stitch which can be worked either at random or in regular patterns.*
Bring needle out at left, and holding thread downwards, insert needle to right. Make a diagonal stitch to the centre and pull through (1). Hold the loop down with a short straight stitch (2). Work a repeat pattern in rows across (3).

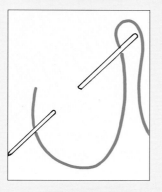  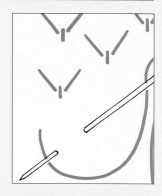

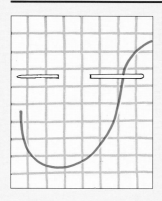 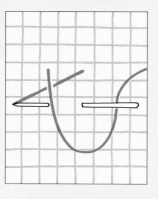 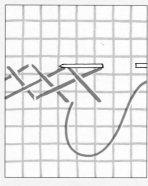

Long Armed Cross Stitch *gives an interesting plaited effect useful for borders and infilling.*
Make a diagonal stitch upwards over two threads and four threads to right. Pass needle behind and bring out two threads to left (1). Make a diagonal stitch downwards over two threads and two to right. Pass needle behind and bring out two threads to left (2). Repeat the sequence to end of row (3).

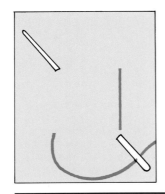 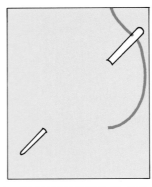 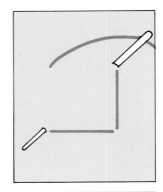

Four-Sided Stitch *Begin on the right. Bring the thread out, then: insert the needle 4 threads up and bring out 4 threads down and to the left (1). Insert needle as shown then bring out at the opposite corner (2). Form the third side of the box, again emerging at the opposite corner (3). Continue in this way to the end of the row. This stitch can also be used as a filling, by repeating the rows.*

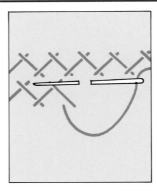 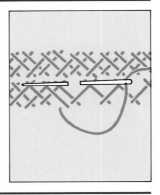

Double Herringbone Stitch *This stitch can be worked on plain and even-weave fabrics and canvas. It consists of a foundation row of basic herringbone with a second row, often a contrasting colour, worked over it.*

Ringed Back Stitch *This stitch is worked from right to left. Bring the thread out, then insert the needle 2 threads down, bringing it back out 4 threads up and 2 to the left. Insert the needle where you started and bring out 2 threads up and 4 threads to the left. Continue creating half-rings in this way following the grid illustrated (1). At the end of the row turn the fabric and backstitch to complete the rings (2).*

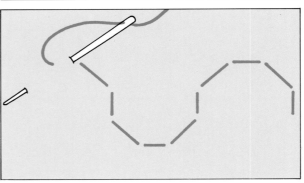

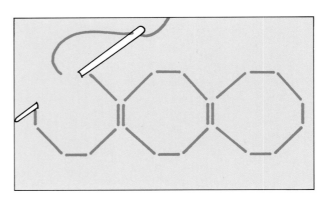

Above *An embroidered Danish family tree, showing both sides of the family of the married couple, their family symbols and their children.*

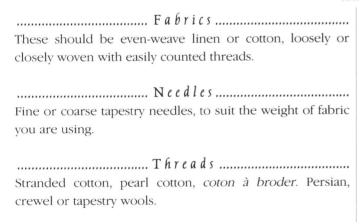

.... *Fabrics* ....

These should be even-weave linen or cotton, loosely or closely woven with easily counted threads.

.... *Needles* ....

Fine or coarse tapestry needles, to suit the weight of fabric you are using.

.... *Threads* ....

Stranded cotton, pearl cotton, *coton à broder.* Persian, crewel or tapestry wools.

CROSS STITCH

This stitch and variations of it have been used all over the world for centuries. Cross stitch is a strong feature of peasant embroidery, the inspiration of the patterns and motifs being the people's surroundings – flowers, animals, birds and trees. The patterns were handed down from generation to generation, often in the form of household items and clothing decorated for weddings or other celebrations. As these would have many hours of work put into them, they were not worn or used as much as every day items and have therefore survived.

The patterns of course are different from one country or region to another, with local preferences for colour and arrangements. Cross stitch is usually worked on even-weave fabric, but where this was not made, the patterns were spaced by eye rather than counted.

Interesting arrangements occurred when patterns did not quite fit the shape of the garment or fabric, leaving the embroiderer completely free from the regularity of mass-produced work.

Cross stitch is a versatile stitch, as it can be used for outlines, solid fillings, motifs and borders. The top diagonal should lie the same way, unless you are experimenting with

51

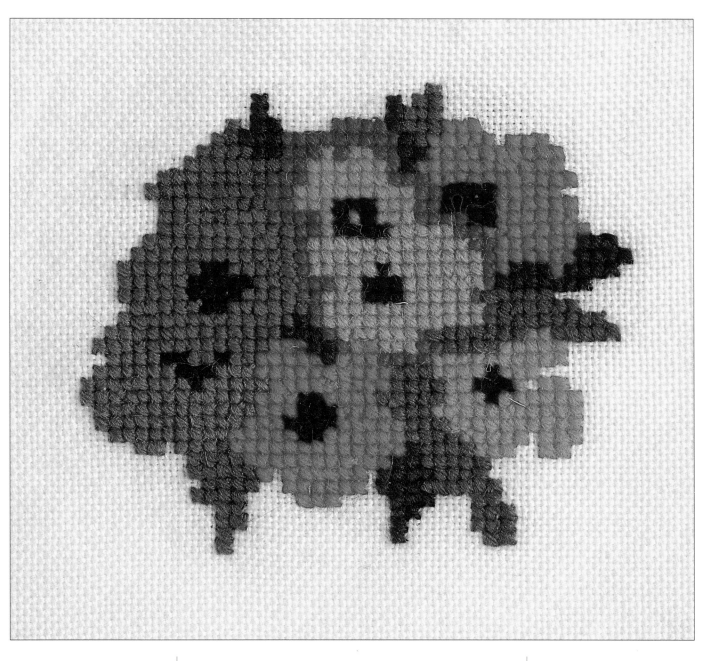

different effects. You can work cross stitches individually, so that a complete cross is made before moving on to the next, or in rows, with the first diagonal of the stitches worked for the whole row, before returning to cover them from the opposite direction.

.... F a b r i c s ....
Even-weave or canvas
Threads – stranded cotton, pearl cotton, soft embroidery cotton, *coton à broder,* crewel wool, Persian wool, tapestry wool.

.... N e e d l e s ....
Tapestry needles.

***Above** Anemones worked in wool on heavy even-weave wool fabric, which makes a very substantial surface. It could be used for a stool top or seat cover if worked over the whole surface.*

Above *The same stitches worked on canvas.*

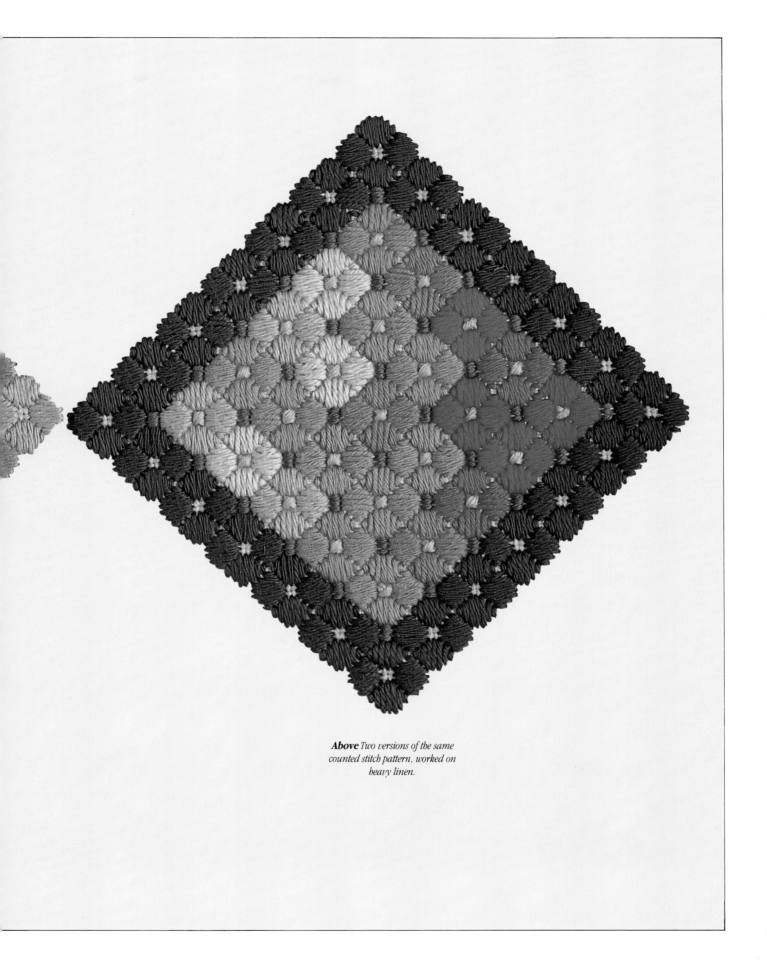

Above *Two versions of the same counted stitch pattern, worked on heavy linen.*

COUNTED CROSS STITCH
HAND TOWELS

Small hand towels specially made to work cross stitch on are available in many needlecraft shops. If you cannot find them near you, the designs can be worked on a strip of even-weave fabric which is then applied to a towel.

To work the towels you need stranded embroidery cottons (for colours, see finished towels), a small tapestry needle and a chart to work from.

To begin, find the centre of the work and mark it with a tacking line vertically, which helps you count the stitches accurately as you work on either side.

Three stands of cotton are used to work the cross stitches. Remember that the top part of the cross should always go in the same direction throughout the work. Try to keep the crosses the same tension for overall neatness.

Any squared paper chart can be used, but make sure before you begin that it will fit the height of your border. Why not make your own counted thread pattern? All you need is squared paper, some coloured felt pens and some ideas. Keep them simple to start with and try them out on a spare piece of even-weave fabric first.

Right *Three hand towels worked with cross stitch inset borders.*

Below *Counted cross stitch on a soft cotton hand towel worked by young women in a co-operative in India.*

Below
Charts for the three towel designs.

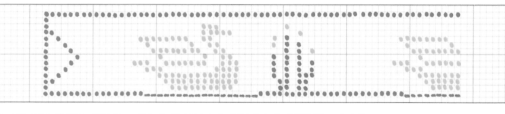

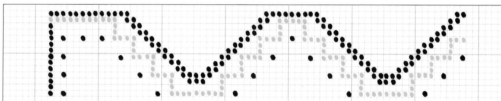

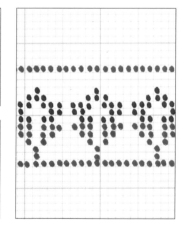

Above *The little house miniature is only 2¹⁄₂in (6.5cm)*
in diameter and is simple enough to be worked in a couple of
evenings. It was designed and worked by a beginner.

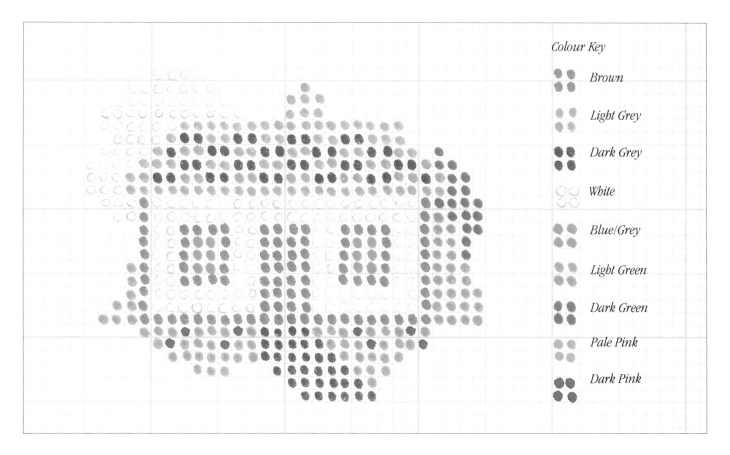

Colour Key

Brown

Light Grey

Dark Grey

White

Blue/Grey

Light Green

Dark Green

Pale Pink

Dark Pink

Although the little house is worked on fine evenweave linen with 29 threads to the inch (2.5 cm), it is quite easy to work, even for a beginner. You can do the same design on larger scale fabrics, but the number of strands of cotton would have to be increased.

For the House Miniature you will need:
A small piece of even-weave linen, 29 threads to the inch (2.5 cm), about 5 in (13 cm) square
Small amounts of stranded cottons in nine colours (as listed on the chart)
A small tapestry needle
An embroidery hoop
A small frame to put the finished work in

Take the fabric and either oversew the edges or use a sewing machine and a zig-zag stitch all round. Mark the centre from top to bottom and sideways with a line of tacking stitches going through the fabric on exactly the same line both ways. Stitches are counted from this, so it is important to be accurate.

Put the fabric into the embroidery hoop and secure it. Look at the chart and identify the symbols for each coloured thread. Starting from the centre and using two strands of brown thread, begin to work the cross stitch for the bottom line of the house. Each stitch goes over two threads both ways. Follow the chart until all stitches are worked. Now work the roses, with stem stitch and tiny French knots for the flowers, and the birds with straight stitches, using one strand of cotton.

If you enjoy doing counted cross stitch embroidery, you might like to make up your own design on squared paper. Perhaps a photograph of your own house or garden could be used. Draw the main shape lightly with pencil on to the paper and then mark each coloured area with a different symbol, just like the little house project. Each stitch should have a small square of the paper to itself – parts you want to outline more strongly can be worked on top of the cross stitch afterwards, with outline stitch. Don't worry too much about a faithful colour match with the real building, use colours that look the most effective with each other. If the design looks a bit isolated, add some clouds or sky, or any other area that will make it 'sit' more substantially. You could finish with the date you worked it and your name; this adds interest and you never know it might become a treasured heirloom!

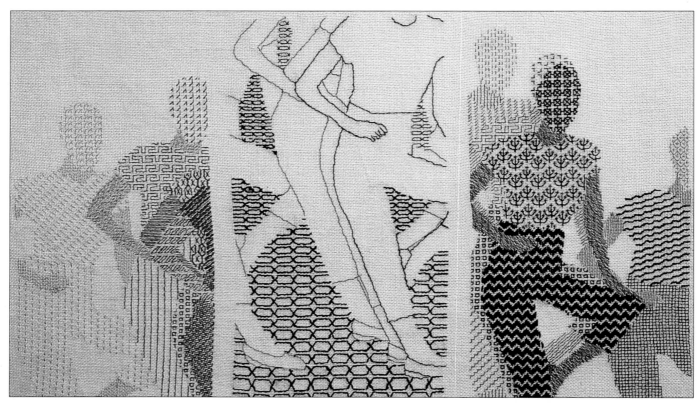

Above This modern example of blackwork worked in red as well as black is based on a repeated design of a figure in action. The variation in tone was achieved using different thicknesses of thread, emphasized by the interplay of stitch patterns. Notice the contrasts created by either outlining or filling in the same basic shape, and the interesting use of colour.

BLACKWORK AND ASSISI

Both these counted thread embroidery techniques are worked on fabric with an even-weave warp and weft that can be easily counted. The stitches are straight and not knotted.

Blackwork is thought to have been brought to England by Henry VIII's first wife, Catherine of Aragon, in 1509, but black counted thread work was known in England long before that date. It was probably due to Catherine's influence that it became popular. Traditionally, this embroidery was worked on very fine linen using fine black silk thread. The designs were naturalistic in form, incorporating scrolls, flowers, leaves and pictorial and geometric patterns. Blackwork was largely a monochrome technique, usually black on a white ground, but sometimes red thread was used, and gold and silver might be added for richness.

The patterns are formed by counting the threads in varying numbers. Traditionally each section was outlined with various stitches. Today we still keep the same patterns that are characteristic, but outlining is no longer obligatory.

The two basic stitches used are double running or Holbein stitch and back stitch. These stitches are used to build up the patterns and repeated for borders or blocks of tone.

Fabrics

These should be even-weave, linen or cotton with easily countable threads. Hessian, wool, hopsack, hardanger fabric (double-weave) or tweeds are all suitable for the background.

Needles

Choose a needle that slips easily between the fabric threads. A blunt-ended needle is suitable between sizes 16 to 26.

Threads

Choose a thread that will not distort the fabric by being too thick. Any sewing cotton can be used, as well as machine embroidery No.50. Stranded cotton, pearl cotton, fine lace threads, silk and fine crewel wools are also suitable.

Practise stitches with a piece of fabric firmly anchored in a hoop or frame. Start each pattern with two or three back stitches which will then be worked over (do not pass threads over empty spaces at the back as they will be visible from the front). Try to get a rhythm and pattern in the way the stitches are worked, to keep them even and neat. Practise putting combinations of stitch patterns together and making some appear darker or lighter by spacing them further apart, or reducing the number of threads you are using if it is possible. You will soon see how to control areas of tone in this way.

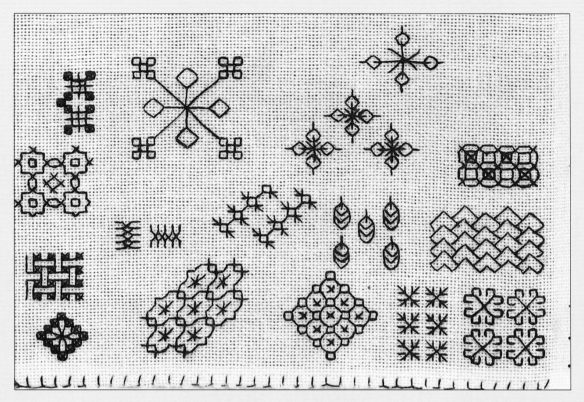

Above *A stitch sampler for blackwork showing some of the many combinations that can be achieved. This sort of worked record of different stitch patterns is invaluable to keep for future reference.*

Left *Horse at the water's edge – this design in blackwork has no outline. The heavy black areas are worked with three strands of cotton, reducing to a single strand on the more open parts.*

61

Above *Starfish and spiders. This very effective design of blackwork stitches is simply highlighted by a gold edge couched around the starfish.*

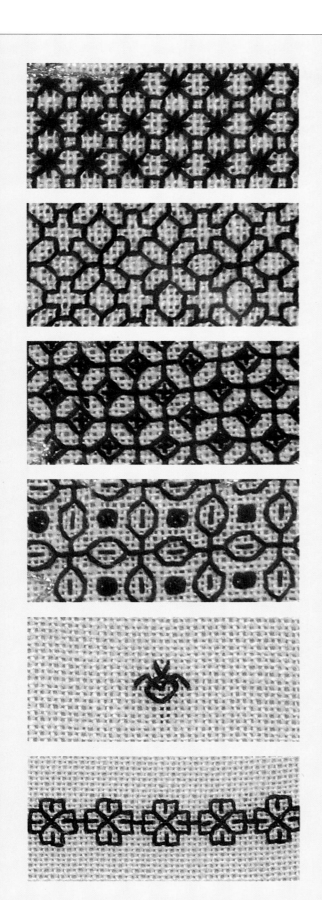

This project is much less complicated than it looks. The stitch used throughout is double running stitch, each stitch worked over two threads or two diagonals. This applies to the different patterns. You can of course choose to sew over three or four threads or diagonals, which will of course increase the size of your design proportionately.

Materials needed:
Coarse even-weave linen (18 in × 14 in (45 cm × 35.5 cm)
black stranded embroidery cotton
gold thread
very fine couching silk

To start the embroidery, oversew the edges by hand or with a zig-zag stitch on a sewing machine to prevent it fraying. With a contrasting sewing thread, tack lines centrally down and across the ground, following the weave. These lines give you a starting point for centring your design. The shapes of the starfish can be accurately traced from the picture or drawn free-hand straight on to the fabric with a soft pencil.

Following the stitch illustrations, and with two strands of cotton, work the bodies of the starfish. The outline is made by couching a thread around the shapes. The spiders can be placed at random. Lastly the border is placed to frame the composition.

The finished piece could be used as the cover of a scrapbook or photo-album with holiday memories in it; embroidered in to the centre of a cloth; or repeated groups of starfish could be made into a cushion. If it was worked on a larger and stronger piece of fabric in bright colours, it could also be made into a simple beach bag.

ASSISI

The Italian town of Assisi gave its name to this form of embroidery, and it was originally used to enrich church linens. Two main stitches are used, double running or Holbein stitch and cross stitch. Long-armed cross stitch was originally used, but most people today use simple cross stitch. The characteristics of Assisi work are that the design is left unworked and the background is filled in with cross stitch, with the motifs outlined in a darker colour.

.... Fabrics ....
Even-weave linens or cottons.

.... Threads ....
Stranded cotton, soft embroidery cotton, pearl cotton and *coton à broder* are suitable. Traditionally, two colours were used – rust or blue with a darker contrast for the outline.

.... Needles ....
Blunt-ended tapestry needles.

Above *A detail from an early example of Assisi work. The stitches used are long-armed cross stitch and back stitch, on a linen ground.*

Right *Detail of Assisi work. The background is worked first, in cross stitch, and the unworked pattern spaces are outlined last in double running stitch. The 'trellis edge' can be placed as desired.*

Above *A place mat recently worked in the town of Assisi, which gives its name to this type of embroidery. The stitches are so neat, it is completely reversible, as you can see from the lower portion of the picture. The pattern is traditional and was the starting point for the piece worked on larger scale Aida (even-weave) fabric.*

Canvas Work

Canvas work is a form of embroidery which covers the canvas on which it
is worked, using stitches that relate to the canvas threads.
Canvas work is often incorrectly called 'tapestry' work, but this
properly refers to woven work. It is now often referred to as needlepoint.
Some stitches which we associate today with canvas work have been
known for hundreds of years, originally worked on even-weave linen.
The most common stitch is tent stitch. The name comes from the
French 'tenter' – to stretch. It refers to stretching the
background fabric on a frame for working. Today
a whole range of stitches are used.

Above *Simple shapes like the ones used in this picture are an ideal base for working experimental stitches. Different thicknesses of threads can be used to give a change of texture. This has been worked in stranded cotton, pearl cotton and tapestry wool.*

.... F a b r i c s ....

Canvas – cotton or linen.

The coarseness or fineness of the canvas mesh is defined by its mesh count eg 10 holes per inch (40 holes per 10 centimetres). As the mesh count gets higher, the canvas gets finer. The count can go from 3½ holes per inch to 24 holes per inch.

There are two basic kinds of canvas, double and single thread. In a single thread canvas (also known as mono), threads are evenly spaced and the holes between them are all the same size. In double thread canvas (also known as Penelope), the rather finer threads are woven in pairs. Interlock canvas is also available. It has double vertical threads woven round a single horizontal thread and does not fray.

.... T h r e a d s ....

Tapestry and crewel wools are the traditional yarns for this work, but any kind of thread can be used as long as it covers the canvas properly but is not so thick that it distorts it. Knitting yarns, silk, raffia, embroidery cottons and silk are a few examples that can be explored.

.... N e e d l e s ....

Tapestry needles – use a size that relates to the canvas size. The needle should be small enough to pass through the spaces between the threads without being forced, and the eye should be large enough to hold the chosen thickness of thread without damaging it. Experimenting will show you what you feel most comfortable with.

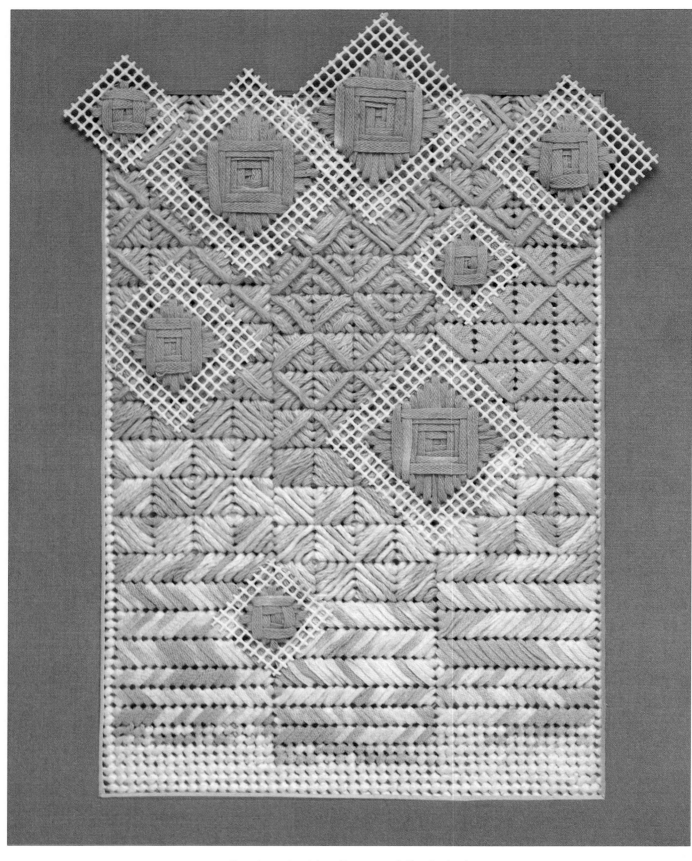

Above *An experimental panel in canvaswork. The cotton hand-knitting yarns were space dyed first. The small squares of canvas on top were worked first and then stitched on.*

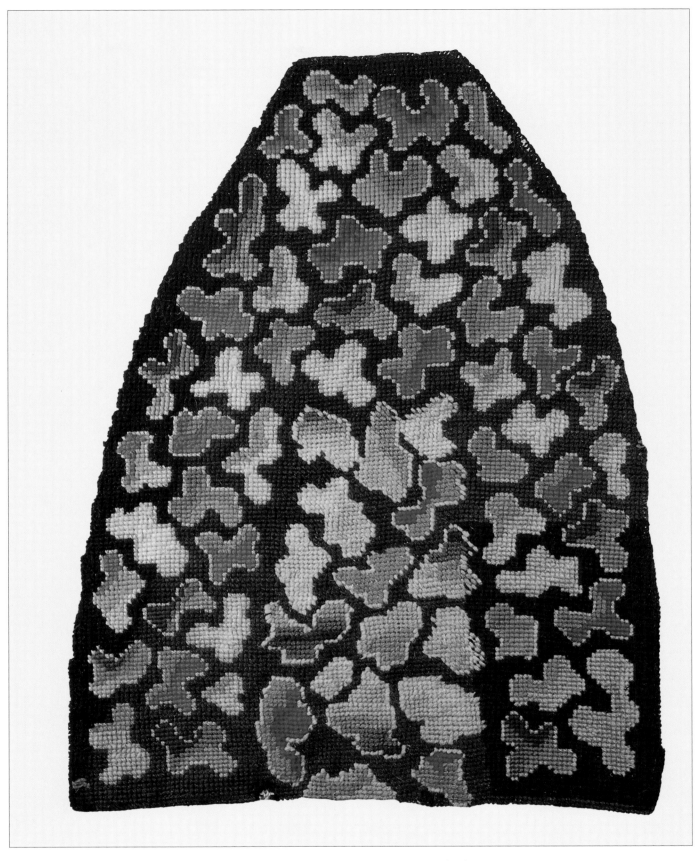

Above *Victorian canvaswork in tent stitch, worked in wool and silk on cotton canvas.*

CANVAS WORK
STITCHES

Gobelin Stitch *(also known as oblique Gobelin stitch) – Gobelin stitch is a canvas stitch used on mono canvas. It makes a smooth surface, which is useful where a flat area of needlepoint is needed to accentuate a more textured stitch. It is similar to tent stitch in appearance and consists of horizontal rows of small slanting stitches. The rows are worked from the bottom of the area to be covered and run alternately from left to right and from right to left. The stitches are two canvas threads tall and slant diagonally over one thread. It is very important to follow this method closely in order to keep the 'pull' of the stitch correct, otherwise the surface will become uneven.*

Long Stitch *is a canvas stitch used on mono canvas. It makes a triangular pattern and has the appearance of a brocaded fabric when worked in a lustrous embroidery thread, such as stranded cotton or silk. Each horizontal row is worked in two journeys, and consists of groups of graduated vertical straight stitches, arranged in triangles. On the second journey, the triangles are reversed and fill in the spaces left on the first journey. Each journey can be made using a different colour and the stitch looks very effective when two shades of the same colour are used. Each double row of triangles is worked over five horizontal threads but the stitch can be made deeper by adding extra graduated stitches to each triangular group.*

Square Satin Stitch *(also known as flat square) – Square satin stitch is a canvas stitch used on mono canvas primarily for filling large shapes and backgrounds. It makes a pattern of diamond shapes, which in turn makes a pattern of large squares when four diamonds are set together. Each diamond shape consists of eleven satin stitches of graduating lengths, with the satin stitches worked either vertically or horizontally. Follow the arrangement of the diamonds and the direction of the stitches shown carefully. This stitch looks extremely attractive when worked on a small scale using pearl cotton or stranded cotton. The light and shade effect created by the different directions of the stitches is accentuated by the lustrous texture of the thread. The diamonds can also be striped in alternating colours: this creates a strong, bold pattern on the surface if two contrasting colours are used, or a much more subtle effect if two close shades of one colour are used.*

Cross Stitch (double) *(also known as* double straight cross stitch*) This is a canvas stitch consisting of a large upright cross overstitched by a smaller cross. It forms raised diamonds and is usually worked over four vertical and four horizontal canvas threads. Work the rows from left to right and then right to left.*

Rhodes Stitch *This is a raised filling stitch which covers a square of canvas with an even number of threads. You work it the same whatever the number of threads making up the square. Follow the numbered arrows; each stitch overlaps the previous stitch until the square is filled. Finish with a small vertical straight stitch at the centre going through the layers of thread and canvas to the back.*

Long armed cross stitch *this stitch is worked from left to right and consists of long diagonal stitches. The long stitches are worked over twice the number of threads as the short stitches.*

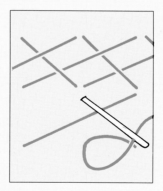

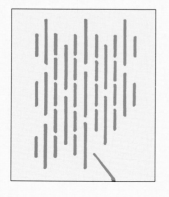

Hungarian Stitch *is used on mono and Penelope canvas. It makes tiny diamond shapes, which can be worked alternately in two colours or used to create a more complex geometric design, using several colours. It also makes a good backround stitch when worked in monochrome. When making a complicated pattern, first work all the stitches of one colour, then all the stitches of the second colour and so on. Each stitch consists of three vertical straight stitches of different lengths to cover two, four and then two horizontal threads of canvas.*

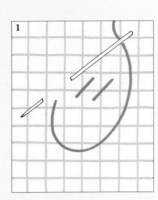
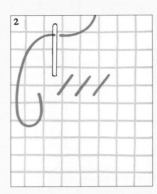
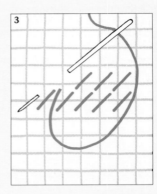

Tent Stitch (Horizontal) *is one of the smallest canvaswork stitches – useful for fine detail, lines or for filling background areas. Because both sides are covered equally well, it is hardwearing and ideal for upholstery. Working from right to left, make a diagonal stitch upwards over one intersection, bring needle out to left of starting point (1). Complete row, insert needle above (2), turn work and repeat the sequence to finish (3).*

Rice Stitch *covers the canvas well and gives a dense, rough texture. Working from right to left, make a cross stitch over two intersections. Bring needle out at centre top. Insert at centre right and bring out at centre bottom (1). Reinsert at centre right and bring out at centre left. Work the other corners in the same way (2). Complete the cross and bring needle out two threads below, ready to make the next stitch (3).*

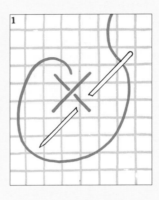
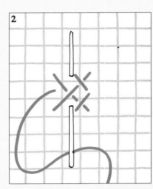
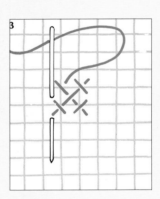

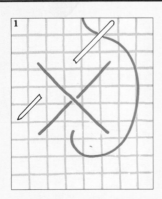
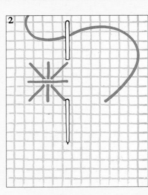
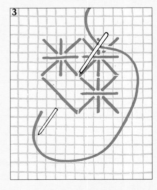

Smyrne Stitch *gives a raised, knubbly texture. Make a cross stitch over four intersections and bring needle out at centre bottom. Insert needle at centre top and bring out at centre left (1). Insert needle at centre right to complete the stitch, and bring out four threads across and two down. Repeat the sequence over four intersections (2). Work subsequent rows in the opposite direction.*

TENT STITCH

This stitch is universally known and used. It is often the first stitch that people learn, as it is easy to do. It was very popular in the 16th and 17th centuries when it covered everything from seats, stools and settees to curtains. When it is worked in wool on a strong linen canvas it makes a very hardwearing fabric; many large old houses have examples still in use that date back hundreds of years. Tent stitch went out of favour for a long time, when people slavishly copied pictures that imitated tapestry. It still has a place in the embroiderer's stitch vocabulary, especially if the colours and patterns used are fresh and modern.

Below *'Tulips'. A picture worked in tent stitch throughout. The flat surface of the stitches does not detract from the strong design.*

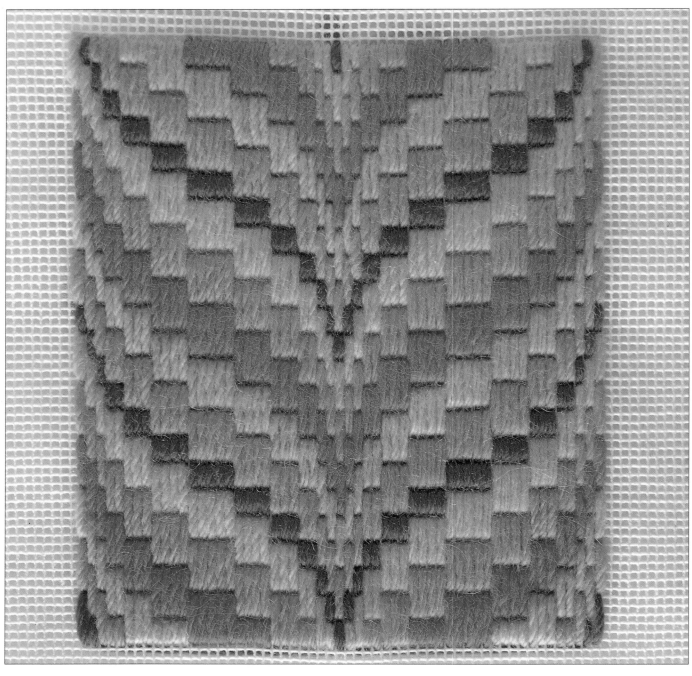

Above *The basic pattern of straight stitches that make up*
Florentine design is clearly visible in this sample.

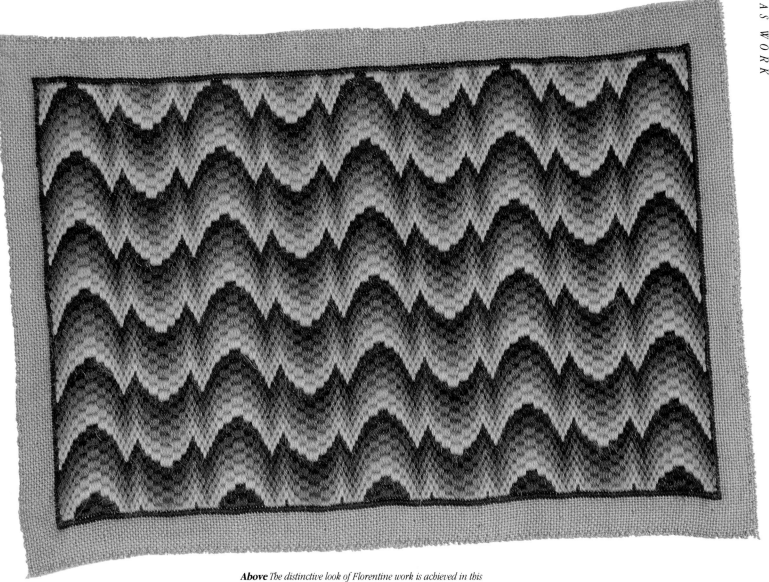

Above *The distinctive look of Florentine work is achieved in this example by using four close-toned grey-blues and two yellows in sequence throughout.*

FLORENTINE

This stitch pattern is popular with embroiders all over Europe and America. The characteristic flame and wavy repeating patterns can be used in many ways and there are hundreds of combinations to choose from. It is generally used to fill large areas, worked in two or more rows of different colours, forming an overall wave pattern. The size of the wave may be varied, depending on the number of stitches and threads being worked on. It is a good exercise to take some squared paper and to draw some patterns of your own. Start with a simple combination, then on the next pattern try stretching the first one out and reversing it for a 'mirror' image. Play about with differing stitch lengths and repeats. You will find it very interesting and quite addictive.

To start working Florentine, put a piece of canvas on to a frame. Select one strong colour and two softer tones of that shade and then choose another colour. Begin to work combinations of the selected colours until you have a pleasing and harmonious effect. The next experiment could be to break all the rules you have just made and use totally clashing colours and see how that works and what visual effect it has made. It is often different from what you anticipated, and you might discover some interesting combinations.

77

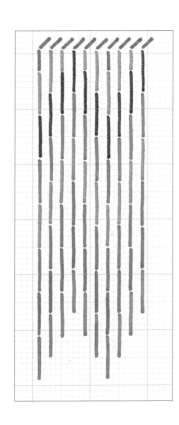

■ *Dark Pink*
■ *Dark Grey*
■ *Light Grey*
■ *Mid Grey*
■ *Pale Pink*

Right *Alternative colours for the tie back.*

Opposite page *Curtain tie back in Florentine embroidery. It is important to work a sample first and look at it from a distance against the curtain to see if the arrangement of the colours is right.*

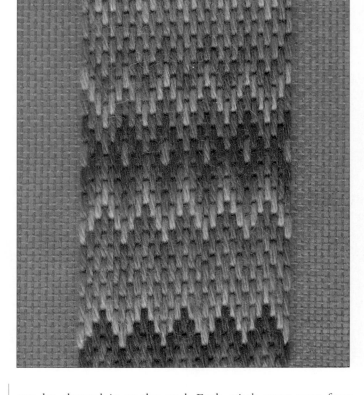

FLORENTINE CURTAIN TIE BACK

You can give your curtains a distinctive look with these Florentine tie backs. They are very simple to do and easy to make up. Build a colour theme around plain curtains or another colour in your room. This design uses five colours, three greys and two pinks. The finished size is 3½ in × 21 in (9 cm × 53 cm), but you can make them any size you want.

You will need (for each tie back):
Piece of canvas, 12 holes to the inch (2.5 cm)
2 skeins of each of five different colours of crewel wool
2 plastic or metal rings, of a size that will go over your back hook
A tapestry needle
Fabric to back the finished work

First bind all the edges of the canvas with masking tape to prevent it fraying while being worked. If you use a frame to work on, stitch the top and bottom of the canvas to the webbing and adjust the tension. It should be firm, so that you get an even surface to the work and it will not need very much pressing to get it square again. Mark the area you are going to work with tacking, which can be removed at the end.

Work the middle row of the pattern (ie pale pink) – start by leaving a 'tail' of about three inches at the back, which can be darned in at the end. Each stitch goes over four threads. When you have worked this first row right across the length, the other rows fit up to it. Finish off with a single row of tent stitch all the way round. When working Florentine stitches, always work in continuous rows; do not change the sequence and work bits here and there as it will not look as neat.

When the embroidery is finished, press it on the wrong side with a damp cloth or steam iron. Leave it to dry completely. Trim off the excess canvas all around the edges, leaving only 1½ in (4 cm). Cut a piece of fabric the same size, to back it (it could be from your curtain fabric). Whatever fabric you use, it should be about the same weight as your canvas work. Turn the edges in all the way round to the finished size of your work and press well. Turn the edges of the canvas in and press down. Place the two pieces together with the right side outwards and pin. With a matching sewing thread and small neat blanket stitches, fasten the pieces together, all the way round. Cover the two rings with buttonhole stitch and double thread, so that they are completely covered. Mark the centres of the ends and attach the rings with several stitches going through the same place. Fasten the thread off securely.

Florentine work can be used in many different ways in the home. You might want to make a matching footstool top or cushions in the same pattern or use plastic canvas to make a small paper bin or plant holder. There are so many uses for this elegant form of work.

Longstitch
A needlecase and cushion front using longstitch patterns.

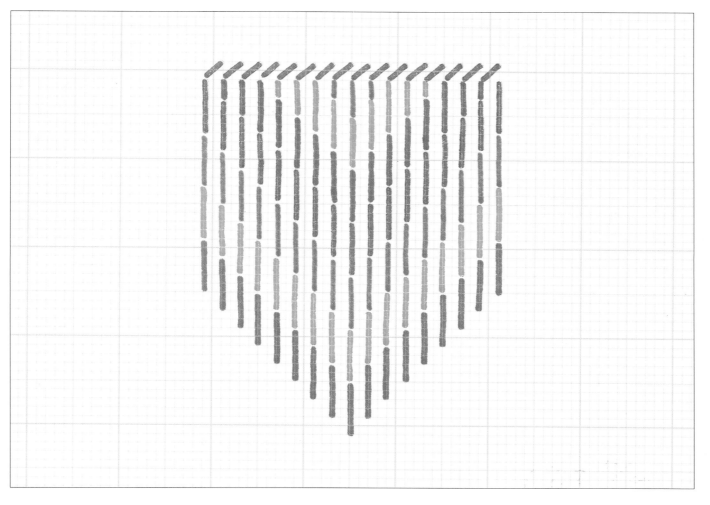

LONGSTITCH

Different stitch effects can be achieved by making long stitches that go over two or more threads in groups. These groups can go in different directions, change colour or yarn texture to make a variety of movements. The designs shown give you some examples you could practice.

LONGSTITCH NEEDLECASE

Finished size 5 in × 3¼ in (13 cm × 8 cm). This is a small, simple project to start you off in canvas work embroidery. The pattern is very easy: once the first horizontal row is worked, all the others just fit in.

You will need:
A piece of 12 holes to the inch (2.5 cm) single thread canvas, about 7 in × 5 in (18 cm × 13 cm)
A tapestry needle
A piece of fabric for the lining, and felt for inside leaves of the needlecase
Small amounts of crewel wools in four colours

Follow the chart and work the first row across the centre of the canvas, having centered the design vertically. Each stitch is made horizontally over 3 threads.

When you have finished working the design, press it on the back with a damp cloth or steam iron.

Cut a piece of lining fabric 7 in × 5 in (18 cm × 13 cm). Fold the edges of the canvas and lining fabric inwards, and buttonhole the two fabrics together neatly around all the edges. Cut two pieces of felt with pinking shears for the inner leaves, make them slightly smaller than the needlecase. Centre them on the inside, stitch a vertical line firmly through all layers – it will look neater if you can 'lose' the stitches in between the canvas work. Make a small button loop on the edge and buttonhole it. Stitch a button on the opposite edge to fasten it.

The canvas stitch pattern for this project can be easily adapted for other items such as cushions and bags. Try out different colour combinations on a spare piece of canvas before you begin the next item; black and white would give a striking effect, or several tones of one colour for a subtle scheme. Other canvas stitches may also be used in toning or contrasting colours.

Left Sample strip in longstitch, showing different colour arrangements, worked in stranded cotton on very fine canvas.

LONGSTITCH CUSHION

This cushions could be worked within two days if you wanted, it is so quick and easy to do. The longstitch used usually goes over more than one thread, so you are covering the canvas at speed! It looks more complicated than it is, the whole square is made up of one quarter repeated in different directions and in different colours. All the patterns and colours are charted here, to work the cushion, but you can do it in any combination you choose. The cushion measures 12½ in (32 cm) square. If you want a smaller cushion, use a finer mesh than the 10 holes to the inch (2.5 cm) used here – perhaps 14 or 16 and a finer thread. For a larger cushion and a chunkier effect, take a larger mesh canvas and double up on the strands of wool.

You will need:
A piece of 10 holes to the inch canvas about 16 in square
14 different colours of Persian embroidery wool or tapestry wool (the amounts needed are given on the chart)
A tapestry needle
A frame if you like working on one
Tape for binding the edges during working

Start by tacking the binding tape all round the edges, which prevents fraying and helps protect the wool from being shredded. Study the chart, of the quarter design. Each square represents a canvas thread. So, if the chart shows three squares of one colour together, it means the stitch goes over three canvas threads. Measure and mark the centre point of the canvas. From this point, work outwards stitching the first line of the design a row at a time (one whole block of the blue and white vertical stitches).

Continue until the first quarter is completed, turn the canvas and begin again from the centre, so that you are stitching the same design in horizontal rows again. Repeat as before until the cushion is completed. Then work the border of cross stitches over two canvas threads in random amounts of crosses, according to the amount of wool you have left. This is optional, but it looks effective and adds to the kaleidoscopic colour. It also eliminates the need to pipe or bead the edge when making up the cushion. The yarn should never be pulled tight – the stitches should remain cushioned and springy.

Hints and tips about working on canvas

Start your work by making a knot in the end of your wool. About two inches away from the starting point of your work take the needle and wool through, leaving the knot on the right side, then continue with the pattern. When you reach the knot you can cut it off, as the thread will be well anchored by then.

When you near the end of the thread, fasten off by running the needle under some stitches at the back.

Small pieces of canvas can be worked in the hand, but you will get a neater more even effect if you work with large pieces on a frame. Cover the piece with a clean cloth pinned to the edges, when not working.

Make sure your hands are really clean before starting work.

Keep the colours you are using separately from others you have and near the work in progress.

Keep the labels from the threads, tie a small piece of the thread through each one, for a quick reference when you need to buy more.

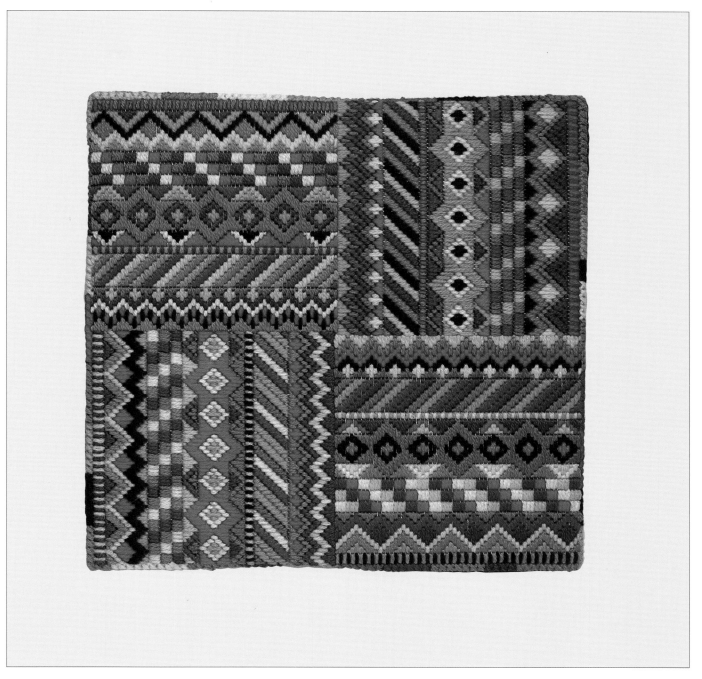

Above *Cushion in longstitch. The same block of pattern has been repeated at different angles four times on the cushion, and the colours changed to emphasise different parts of the pattern.*

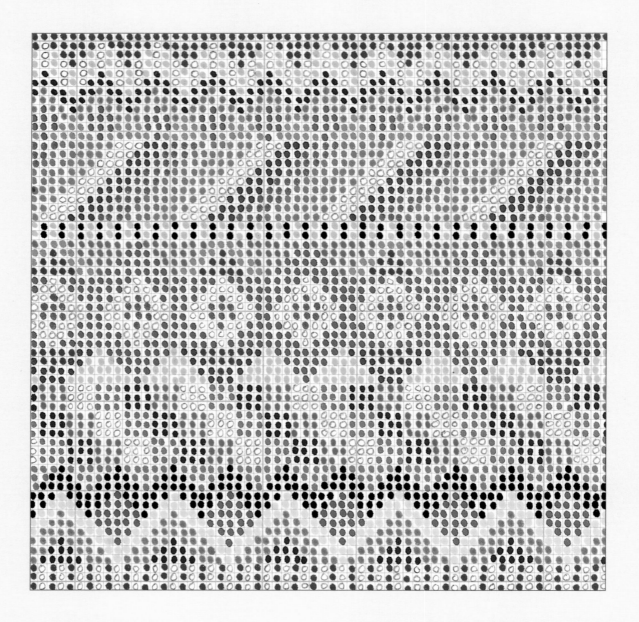

CODE NUMBER OF COLOURS PATTERNA PERSIAN YARN	542	260	340	633	761	971	221	812	353	685	771	301	592	671
QUANTITY OF SKEINS REQUIRED	2	2	2	1	1	2	2	2	2	2	1	2	2	1

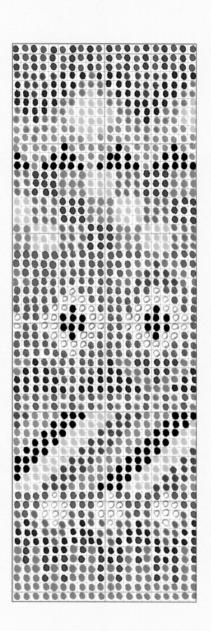
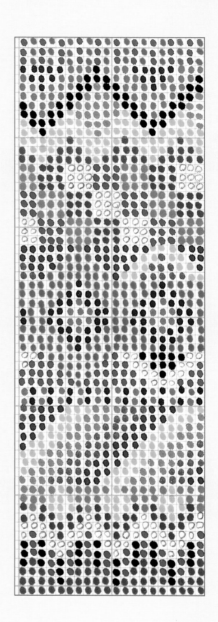

Above *Florentine design based on a shell. The finished piece will have the outline of the shell shape worked in a light coloured wool to make it stand out from the background.*

CREATIVE CANVAS WORK

There are so many different canvas stitches and combinations to choose from, it is difficult to decide which ones to learn first. Practise as many stitches as you can and when you have a few favourites try putting them together in a free way on a piece of canvas, changing the colour, scale or direction as you please. This could be your version of the traditional sampler.

For extra texture and surface interest, try working stitches on top of each other, ie large-scale cross stitch on top of tent stitch, either in the same colour or a contrasting or complementary colour.

Some of the stitches in the counted thread area might appeal to you, so why not try those as well? A change of canvas size and different yarns to work with can also stimulate you to look at the stitches with a fresh eye and to work on new pattern combinations.

Above 'Decadence': a series of designs inspired by 'Vogue' posters from the 1920s. The printed canvas. It could be worked completely in tent stitch with silver thread used on the jewellery.

Above This version of the finished design is worked in a variety of stitches, mostly brick stitch and satin stitch.

Above and right Boxes in embroidered plastic canvas are quick and easy to make, and a good way of learning and practising canvas stitches.

PLASTIC CANVAS

Plastic canvas is available in most needlecraft and craft shops – it is a useful modern addition to embroidery. It has several features which make it attractive to beginners; the mesh is fixed and not easily distorted with tight stitches. It doesn't need pressing or blocking like conventional canvas. The holes are usually larger and clearer than standard canvas, which makes it suitable for beginners, children and those with poor eyesight. Many different threads and stitches can be used to great effect on this canvas, not only regular threads, but hand knitting yarns, raffia, fine ribbons and decorative metallic threads. To finish off the edges of plastic canvas you need a good covering stitch, quite often this is long armed cross stitch. It looks neat and can be used to join sections together.

Lots of different useful things can be made with plastic canvas – boxes, spectacle cases, small litter bins, tissue box covers, place mats, napkin rings etc. Boxes are particularly successful: they are quite stable, even without being lined, and they are quick to make. Both boxes in the project here were made from one standard sheet of canvas (11 in × 14 in/28 cm × 35.5 cm) with 6 holes to the inch (2.5 cm). There are other sizes and shapes available, with different hole counts. When you are working with plastic canvas, mark the dimensions with a ball point pen or marker and cut between the squares, then trim off the projecting spikes back to the main stem. Gather the cut off bits meticulously and throw them away before they get into the carpet or the dog! They seem to get everywhere.

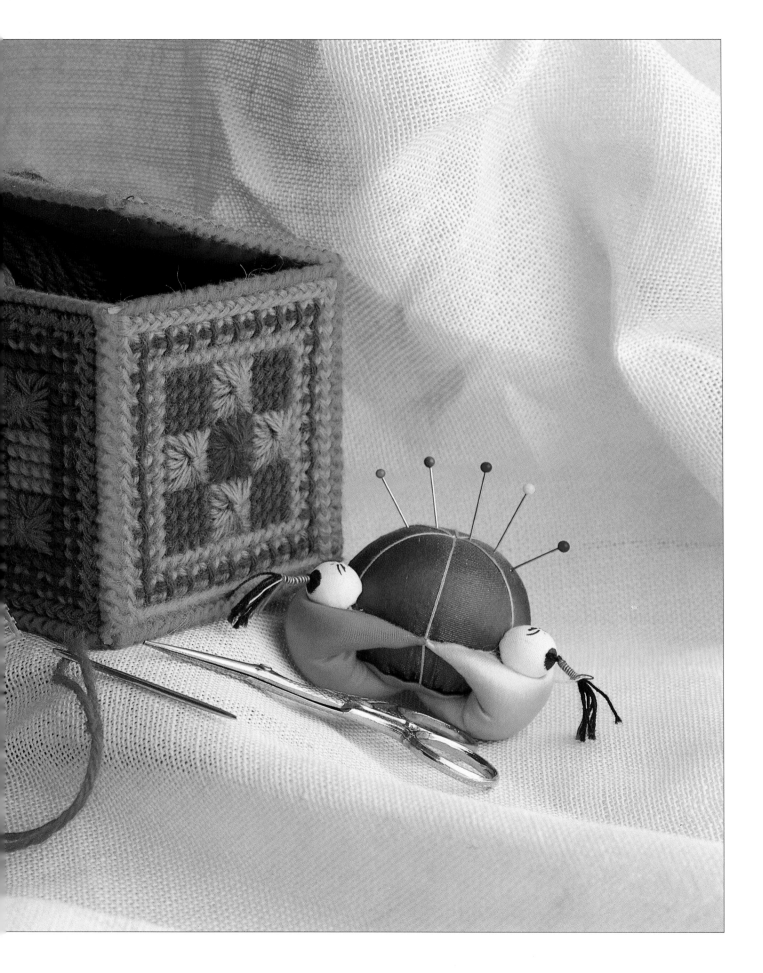

Both boxes are made in exactly the same way, the smaller box has metallic embroidery thread on the Christmas bauble and is worked in cross stitch. It could be used to contain a gift or given on its own. The larger box is worked in different stitches – Rhodes stitch is used to give an extra raised dimension. This box is big enough to get basic sewing equipment in. It would make a lovely gift, lined and filled with threads, needles, a small pair of scissors and perhaps a tape measure.

To make the largest box – finished size 3½ in (19 cm) square
Cut 6 squares measuring 3½ in (9 cm) in plastic canvas 6 holes to the inch (2.5 cm)
2 skeins in each of 5 colours of crewel or tapestry wool
1 skein coton à broder *in a suitable colour for the edges*
1 large tapestry needle

The charts give two pattern combinations which are used alternately for the sides. Choose one for the lid. The chart key gives suggested stitches: practise them first. The colour combinations are up to you, but remember you need two sides the same and three others that match. The base needs to be worked in flat stitches, such as tent stitch or Gobelin stitch.

Begin by working a row one square in all round the first side. Now work the rest of the pattern. When all the sides plus the top and bottom are finished, you should have a raw edge of one unworked square on all sides. Using the *coton à broder* and long armed cross stitch, join the squares together for the main body, alternating the different patterns. Position the base and join it to the main body.

Work long armed cross stitch around three sides of the top before joining it to one top edge of the box.

If you want to line the box, cut six pieces of fabric about 4½ in (11.5 cm) square. Stitch five pieces into the main box shape, wrong sides outwards. Drop the lining into the box, press it into the corners, turn in the top edge and catch stitch into position as neatly and invisibly as you can. For the lid lining, press under the extra fabric all round, pin it in position and catch stitch all round.

The smaller box – finished size 2½ in (6.5 cm) square

This is made in the same way as the larger box. Follow the chart and work the pieces. The gold metallic thread is used to outline the two Rhodes stitch squares, by backstitches through the mesh around the squares. A length of thread is fastened through the top of the bauble and tied in a bow.

LARGE BOX CHART

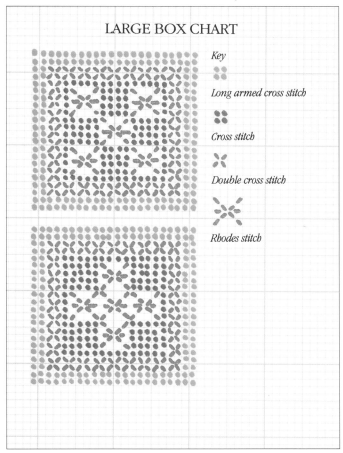

Key

Long armed cross stitch

Cross stitch

Double cross stitch

Rhodes stitch

SMALL BOX CHART

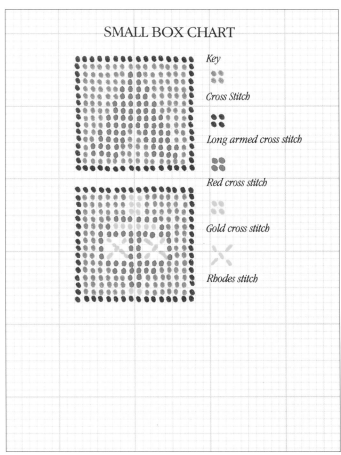

Key

Cross Stitch

Long armed cross stitch

Red cross stitch

Gold cross stitch

Rhodes stitch

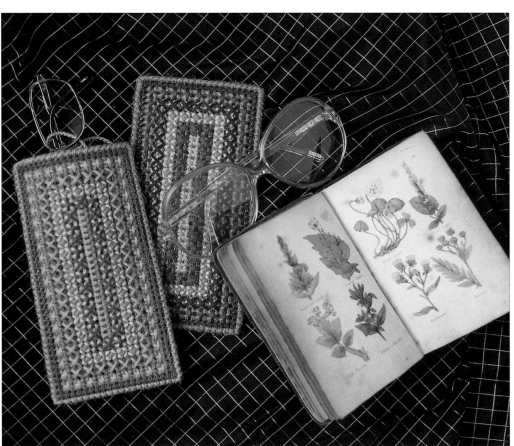

Left *Plastic canvas is ideal for spectacle cases as it is firm and yet flexible enough to take fairly bulky spectacles. If the work is neatened off completely on the back, the case will not need lining.*
A variety of simple stitches have been used on these, including cross stitches on top of each other but in different colours and in different directions.
The two halves are worked separately, leaving the last hole all round the edges free. The pieces are then joined together using long-armed cross stitch.

Opposite page *This small box was worked to put a Christmas gift in it. The pattern of the Christmas bauble could be repeated on all sides if desired, but not on the base.*

Right This chart corresponds to the partly-worked sample in the photograph.

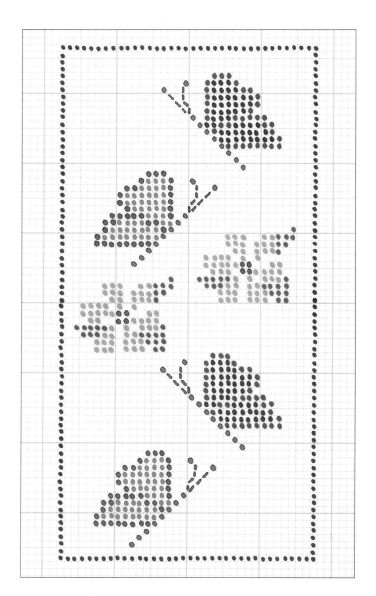

.... Spectacle case in Tent Stitch ....

If you decide to make a spectacle case using this pattern, measure an existing one for size, allowing at least 1½ in (4 cm) of spare canvas all the way round. When you work the pattern, do remember to reverse it on the opposite side, otherwise the butterflies will be flying upside-down.

When the work is complete, press on the wrong side before making up. Join the two sides (on the wrong side) with a firm back-stitch as close as possible to the last stitches. Trim off the excess of canvas and neaten the edges before turning to the right side. Make the lining bag to the same size and, leaving it inside out, place it inside the completed case. Turn in the top edges and neatly slip-stitch the two top edges together.

This pattern, if repeated, could be used for a decorative bell-pull, the mount for a picture frame, perhaps containing pressed flowers or grasses.

Above *The grey spectacle case has been worked in tent stitch with silver highlights. Another example on the top shows how changing the scale and colours gives a totally different effect.*

.... Enlarging and Reducing Designs ....

The artworks in this book have been reproduced as close to actual size as possible, but you may need to enlarge or reduce designs to suit your needs. The designs can be traced off the page and then the image can be enlarged or reduced by a professional copy company, or, if this is unavailable or you prefer to do it yourself, follow the technique shown in the diagrams.

The method shown is for enlarging the diagrams; if you need to reduce a design, simply reverse the process.

1   Trace or draw your design on to the centre of a piece of paper.

2   Draw a small grid pattern over the design, with lines about ¼ in (0.5 cm) apart.

3   Using a straight edge, mark the outer proportions of the shape on the grid.

4   Place the grid on a larger piece of paper and tape down the lower left hand corner. Draw in a diagonal line from corner to corner of the design box, extending beyond the top right hand corner of the grid.

5   Extend the bottom line of the design box to the desired width of the enlargement. Draw a line at right angles from this base line to meet the diagonal.

6   Draw in the top line to meet the left hand side of the grid.

7   Remove the grid and complete the lines in areas covered by the original design.

8   Taking the original grid, number the squares across the width and down the sides.

9   Divide the larger box into the same number of squares as the small grid.

10 You can now reproduce the design by copying the lines from each square of the small design to the corresponding squares on the larger grid.

11 An accurate method of drawing up the image is to mark where each line intersects a grid line and then join the marks.

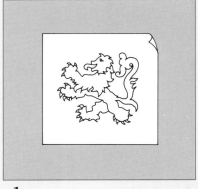

1

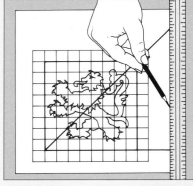

5

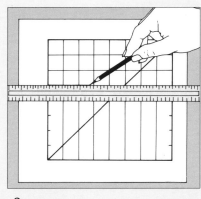

9

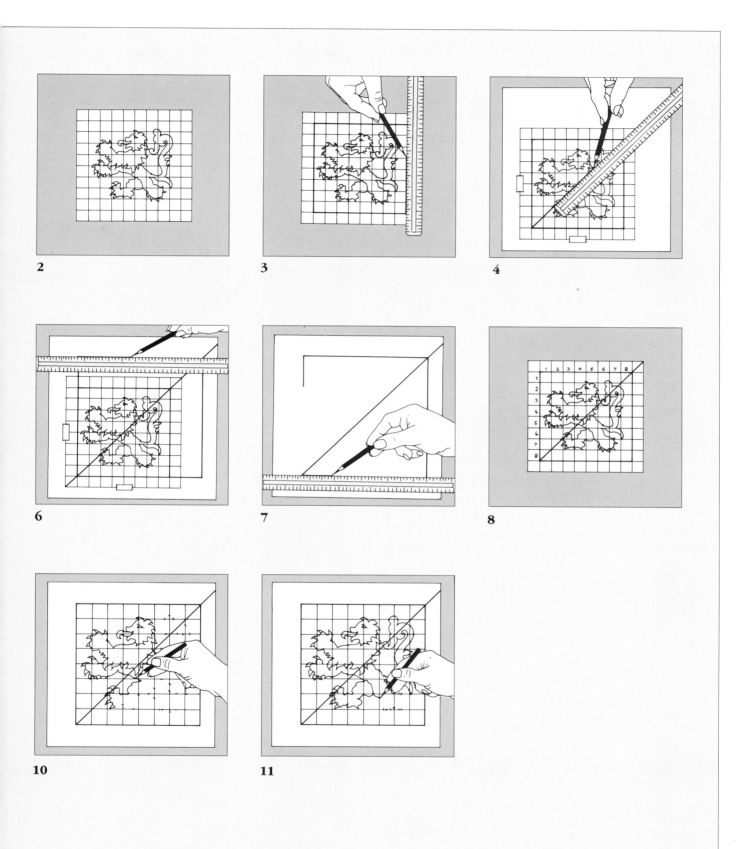

2

3

4

6

7

8

10

11

INDEX

Page numbers in *italics* refer to relevant captions